OCEAN ACCESS

THE **BEACHFRONT TOWNS** OF **MONMOUTH & OCEAN COUNTY** NEW JERSEY

RICH ROMANO

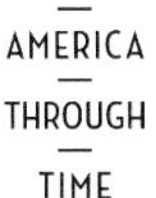

This book is for Christopher and Vincent
may you always enjoy, appreciate, and respect the sea.

AMERICA THROUGH TIME®
An imprint of Sutton Publishing Inc.
www.through-time.com

First published 2025
Copyright © Rich Romano 2025

ISBN 978-1-63499-558-0

Typeset in 10pt on 13pt Sabon
Printed and bound in England

CONTENTS

Introduction   5

  1   Monmouth County   7
  2   Ocean County   48

Select Bibliography   94
About the Author   96

INTRODUCTION

Anyone who has grown up or lived on the Jersey Shore knows the place is unique

Bruce Springsteen

Growing up in North Jersey in the '80s and '90s, I was lucky enough to spend most of my summers on the Jersey Shore. After moving south from Bloomfield, my maternal grandmother lived in a house on 3rd Avenue in the West Belmar section of Wall Township. Once school ended, my brother and I stayed at her house all summer until football practice started in mid-August. Even though we were not, we felt like "locals" for those two and half months. Fond memories of Belmar from those years include: boogie-boarding at the 19th Avenue beach, miniature golf on the boardwalk, spending millions (ok, $20!) at Belmar Playland arcade, hunting for crabs and other wildlife in the algae-covered jetties, shopping at Eastern Lines, fishing on our cousins' boats in Shark River, enjoying a milkshake at McDonalds on the boardwalk and savoring the first frozen yogurt I ever had at TCBY in the "shack" on 19th Avenue. As far as one could see, the beach was full of Romanos, Scaturros, and Iacobellis of all ages. During my college and early professional years, the boys from Belleville (my high school friends) and I would rent houses each summer in Belmar where we spent every Friday night through Sunday afternoon. Beverages were had at Paddy Mac's, Bar A, Paul's Tavern, D'Jais, the Tropical Pub, and the occasional trip to the Headliner in Neptune.

While most of the summer was spent in Belmar, one week in early August was spent at Ortley Beach. My paternal great-grandparents were the first to rent tiny bungalows here, setting in motion five generations of Romanos and Giammarinos vacationing in Ortley over the ensuing decades. Long summer days would be spent on the beach body surfing, diving over the breakers to catch a football, chanting from the sea to get the women into the water and having an afternoon cigar down by the water, listening to a Yankees game on the radio. Nights were spent on the Seaside Heights boardwalk, playing wheels and enjoying rides and Kohr's Frozen Custard. When we didn't go to the boards, we would play cards at the house or simply end the night sitting in a large circle on the Jersey Shore gravel outside our door, telling stories and laughing until 1 a.m.

Other wonderful traditions over the years include: plenty of fishing—party boats out of Leonardo and Belmar or surf fishing just about everywhere for bluefish, stripers, and fluke; concerts at the Fastlane and Stone Pony in Asbury Park; the boardwalk in Point

Pleasant; exploring Sandy Hook's rich history; and, of course, introducing our kids to many of these same traditions which still continue today.

Traveling south on the Garden State Parkway, after the "bridge" around mile marker 122, you pass through Cheesequake State Park—an open, flat section of marsh on both sides. My personal tradition while cruising along this stretch is to roll down all the car windows and replace the depressing North Jersey air with the soothing saltwater sea breeze, until we reach the tree line (mile marker 120). Everyone's hair is now disheveled, but there's a new, positive feeling in the car for the rest of the trip; I call it "the air exchange."

Ocean Access includes original photos and a brief history of every town in Monmouth and Ocean County which touches the Atlantic Ocean. While there are plenty more towns that are part of the seashore (Brielle, Lake Como, Barnegat, Rumson, etc.) or bayshore (Keansburg, Atlantic Highlands, Keyport, etc.), these towns are not situated directly on the ocean. Enjoy the journey!

1
MONMOUTH COUNTY

Although Monmouth County officially starts in Aberdeen along the Raritan Bayshore, the first beach to touch the Atlantic Ocean is fifteen miles away. After traveling east along Route 36 South through what feels like 100 red lights, the highway veers left through Middletown, then up the wooded slopes of Atlantic Highlands, then finally through Highlands on its march to the sea. Suddenly, the tree line ahead vanishes and the gates of paradise appear in the form of the Captain Joseph Azzolina Memorial Bridge. At the apex of the roadway, high above the currents of the Shrewsbury River, the endless blue ocean comes into view, and it looks as if the end of the bridge empties into the water! Luckily, the highway continues on a thin stretch of land, with Sea Bright to the south and Sandy Hook to the north, and, for the purpose of this book, is where our Monmouth County beaches truly begin.

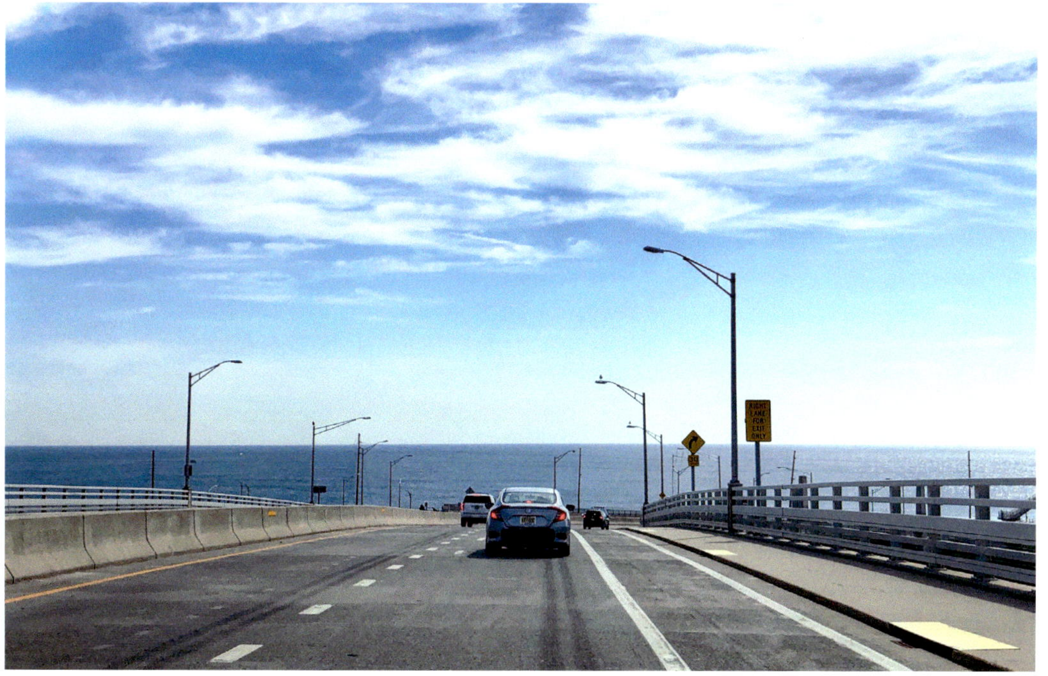

SANDY HOOK

Incorporated: 1798 (as part of Middletown Township)
Motto: none
Origin of the name: From the Dutch "Sant Hoek" meaning "spit of land."

Sandy Hook is owned by the federal government and is managed by the National Park Service. It is part of the Gateway National Recreation Area, together with the shorelines of Jamaica Bay (Brooklyn & Queens) and Staten Island. In fact, the tip of Sandy hook is less than 18 miles from New York as the seagull flies over the bay. The area boasts three public beaches (North, Gunnison & South) along with the remnants of post-civil war forts and batteries.

Europeans first landed in the Sandy Hook area of Middletown around 1609, when explorer Henry Hudson supposedly anchored off these shores. The Dutch East India Company chartered him to find a trade route with Asia, known as the Northwest Passage, connecting the Atlantic and Pacific Oceans (which would not be discovered until 1850). The first structure built on Sandy Hook was the lighthouse in 1764 by the Colony of New York to help ships navigate the tricky waters of Hudson Bay. Then known as the New York Lighthouse, Sandy Hook Light is the nation's oldest working lighthouse.

A fort was needed to protect the harbor, so construction on one began in 1857, but was halted shortly after the end of the Civil War. Between 1874 and 1895, the Sandy Hook Proving Grounds and artillery batteries at Fort Hancock were constructed and reinforced. The fort was redesigned as part of the Endicott Program, which called for "disappearing guns" that could be raised and lowered within the thick walls of the fort. By 1909, there were a total of eighteen batteries housing fifty-one guns.

Still standing are twenty-one buff-brick houses collectively known as "Officers Row." Built in the 1890s, these two-story buildings housed officers and their families. Except for a few private areas, the park is open to the public year-round. Today, Sandy Hook offers 6 miles of free beaches, paved bike paths, excellent fishing, and plenty of opportunity to explore both the ocean and bay sides.

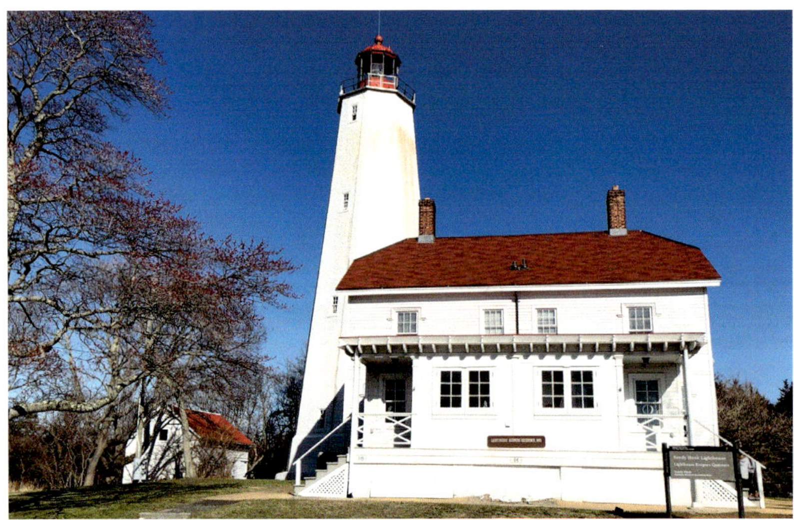

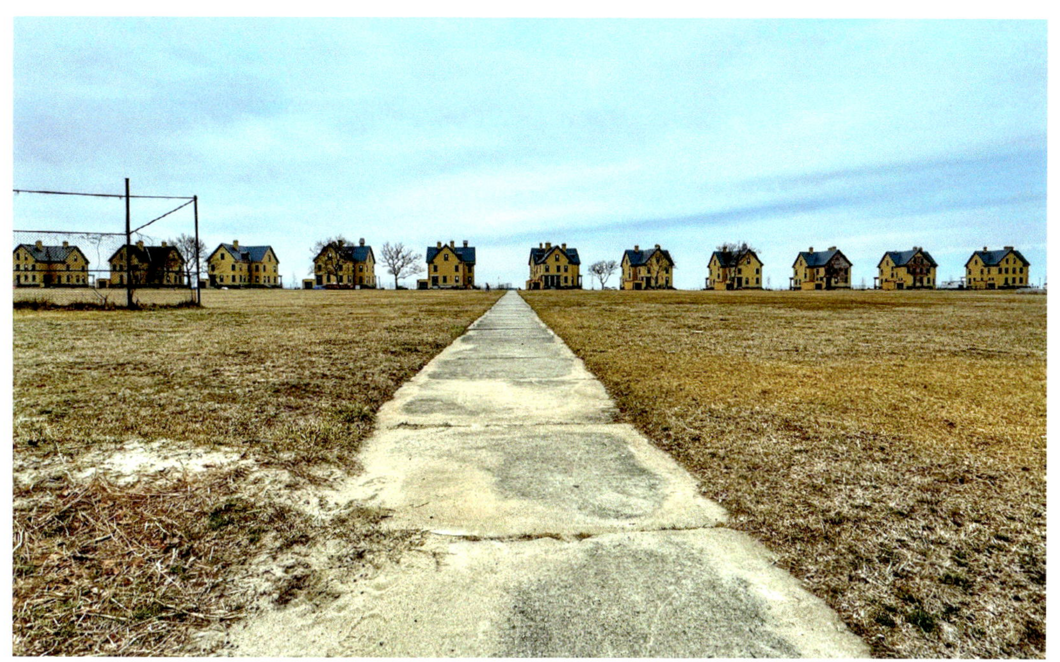

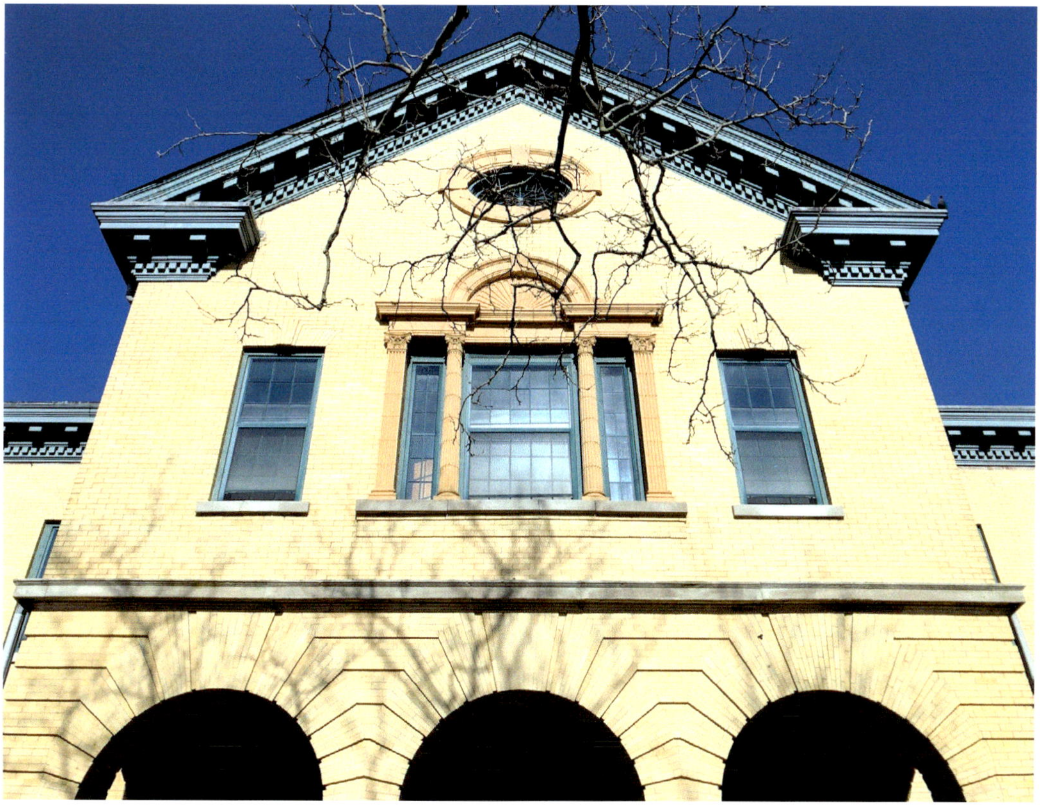

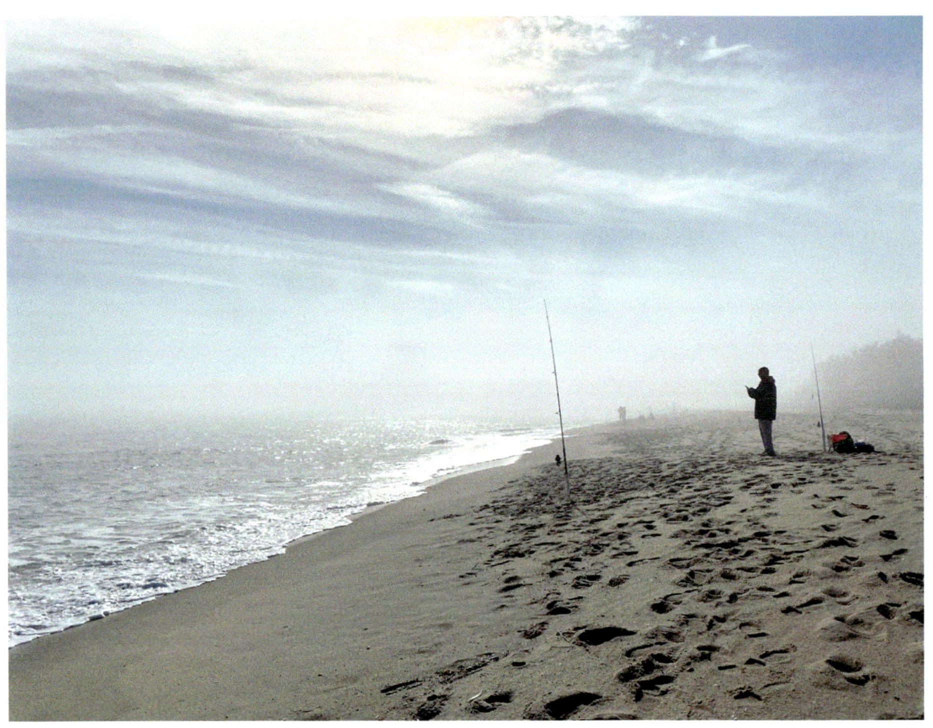

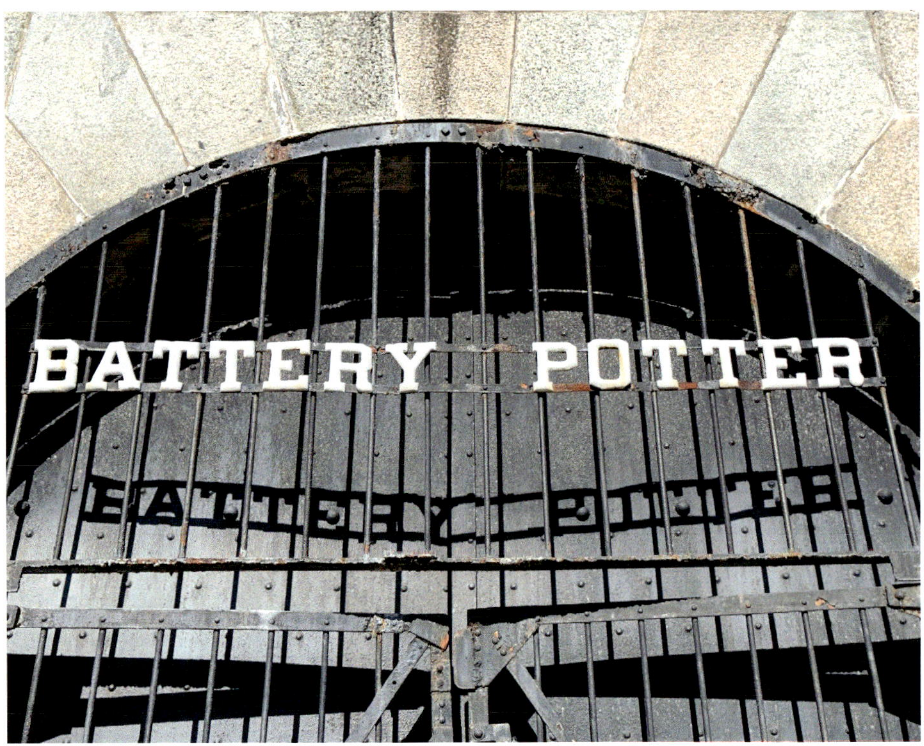
BATTERY POTTER

SEA BRIGHT

Incorporated:	1889
Motto:	"There's no place like Sea Bright"
Origin of the name:	Originally known as "Nauvoo," the Hebrew word for "pleasant place," possibly named after a visit by Joseph Smith in 1840, founder of the Mormon religion.
Formed from:	Portions of Ocean Township

By the middle of the nineteenth century, Sea Bright was no more than a handful of fishing shacks for roughly fifty people along the coast. The Jersey Shore's first hotel, the Ocean House, opened in 1842, about a mile north of today's Sea Bright-Rumson bridge. By 1877, it was known as the Hotel Bellevue; later, the Normandie. The first bridge connecting Sea Bright to the mainland was constructed in 1870. After several iterations, a new bridge is in the works, scheduled to open in 2025. By the end of the nineteenth century, Sea Bright was the largest fishery on the East Coast.

All the land from Sea Bright to Monmouth Beach was originally part of Wardell's Beach, owned by Eliakim Wardell. His descendants sold the land to Dr. Arthur Conover of Freehold for $30,000 in 1865. Later, in 1869, Mifflin Paul purchased the 0.25-mile-wide Sea Bright acreage from Conover, and with railroad expansion and the new bridge to the mainland, Sea Bright began to develop. The Sea Bright Skiff was invented here and was akin to a modern-day lifeguard boat; launched from the surf, through the waves, out to the fishing grounds, and back into the beach with the bounty of the day.

One of the most unique features of Sea Bright is the "seawall" which stretches nearly 5 miles along Ocean Avenue from Sea Bright to Monmouth Beach. It was first constructed in the 1870s in the early years when the area first became a resort and has been rebuilt numerous times. From 1870 to 1950, the New Jersey Southern Railroad and Central Railroad operated a train trestle adjacent to the seawall between Sea Bright and Sandy Hook. By 1950, the state decided not to take over the land after the railroad abandoned the property. Much of the area ended up with private landowners and even to this day, many of the seawall's stairs and decks remain private, while the beach is, and always has been, public.

Today, Sea Bright offers plenty of fun and lively restaurants, exclusive beach clubs, bars and shopping in the center of town.

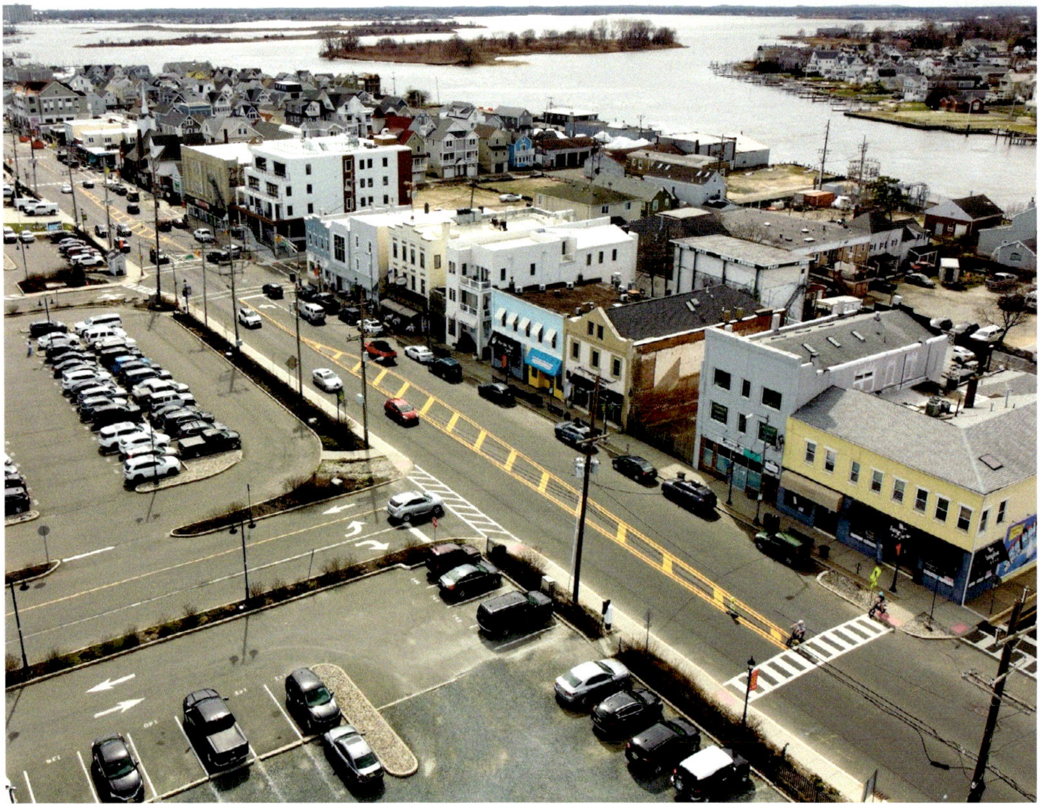

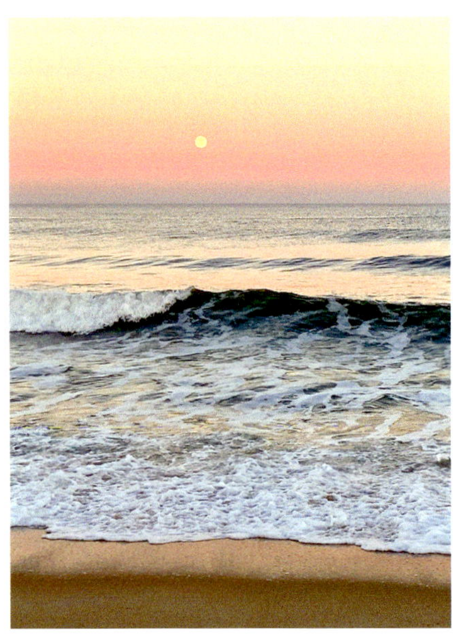

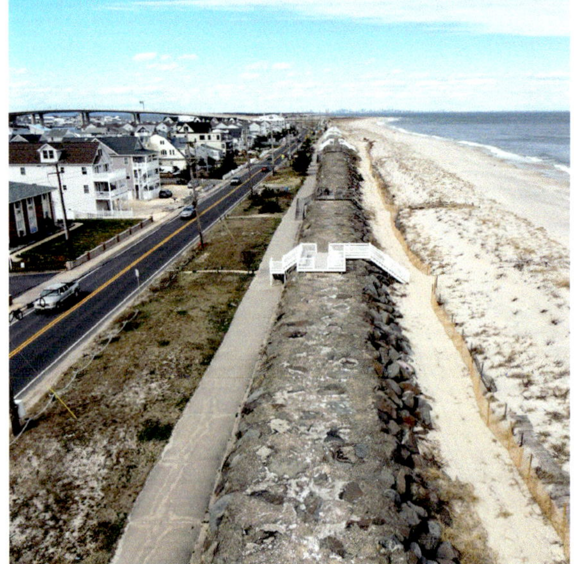

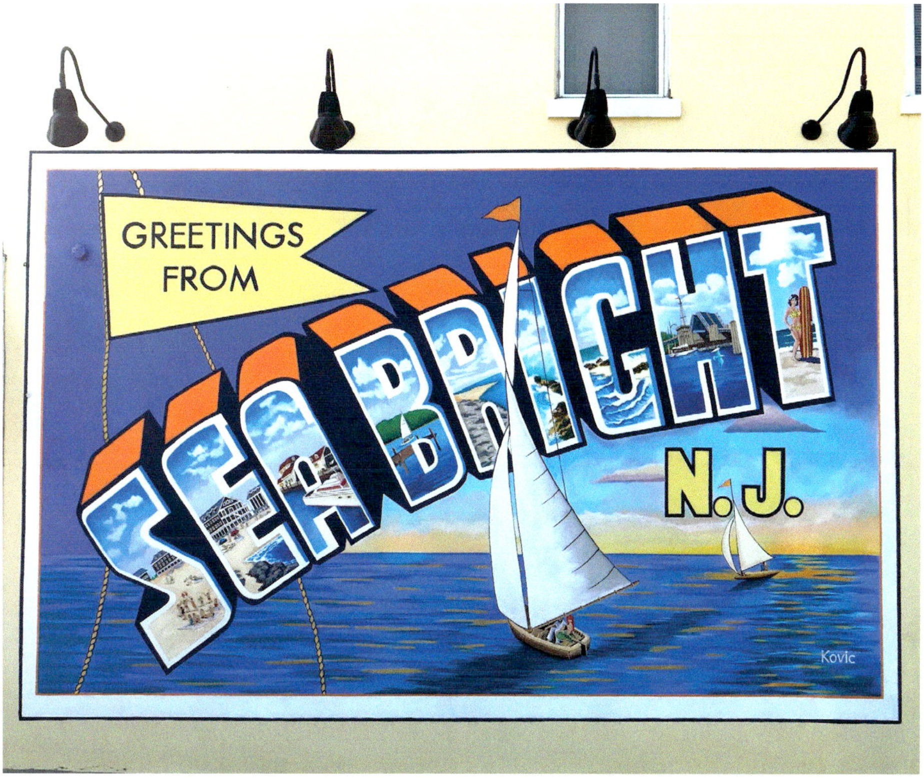

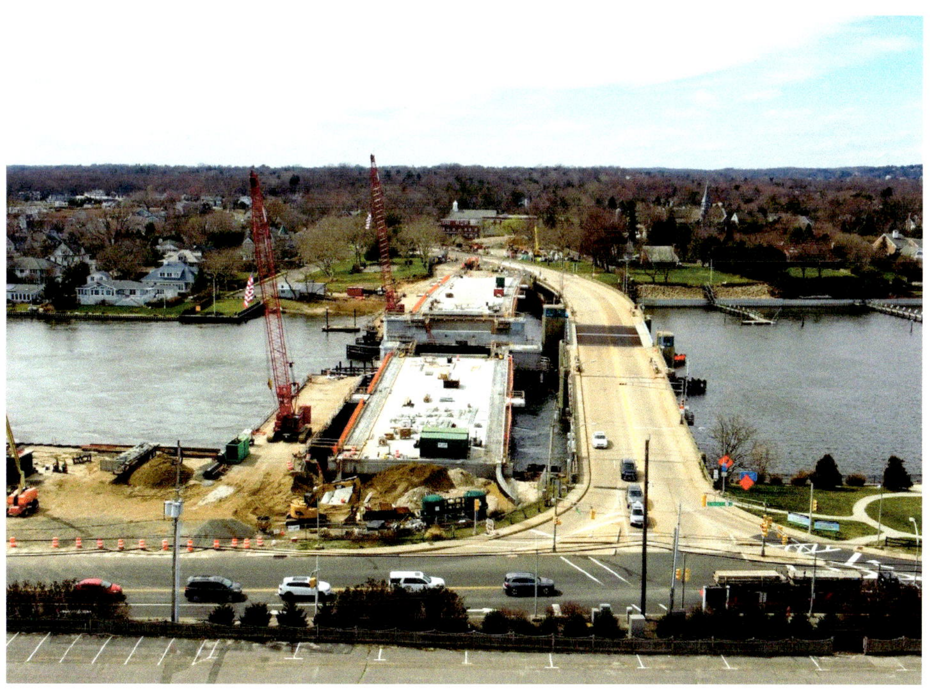

GREETINGS FROM
SEA BRIGHT
N. J.
Kovic

MONMOUTH BEACH

Incorporated:	1906
Motto:	"Seaside Living Since 1906"
Origin of the name:	Named after the county seat Monmouthshire, Wales, or Rhode Island Monmouth Society
Formed from:	Portions of Ocean Township

In 1863, a charter was given to the Long Branch & Sea Shore Railroad which allowed for the East Coast elite to safely travel back and forth to their summer "cottages" in Sea Bright, Monmouth Beach, and Long Branch. These wealthy residents required beach clubs, so in 1910, the Monmouth Beach Bath & Tennis Club (aka "Big Monmouth") opened, followed by the Monmouth Beach Bathing Pavilion (aka "Little Monmouth") in 1921. During this time, Ocean Avenue was known as "Millionaires Row," with houses belonging to the rich and famous, including Jay Gould, John Barrymore, William Fargo, Garret Hobart, and Guglielmo Marconi. Although Monmouth Beach is slightly quieter than its neighboring towns of Sea Bright and Long Branch, it still boasts great beaches, restaurants, and plenty of waterfront views along Manhasset Creek and Shrewsbury Bay.

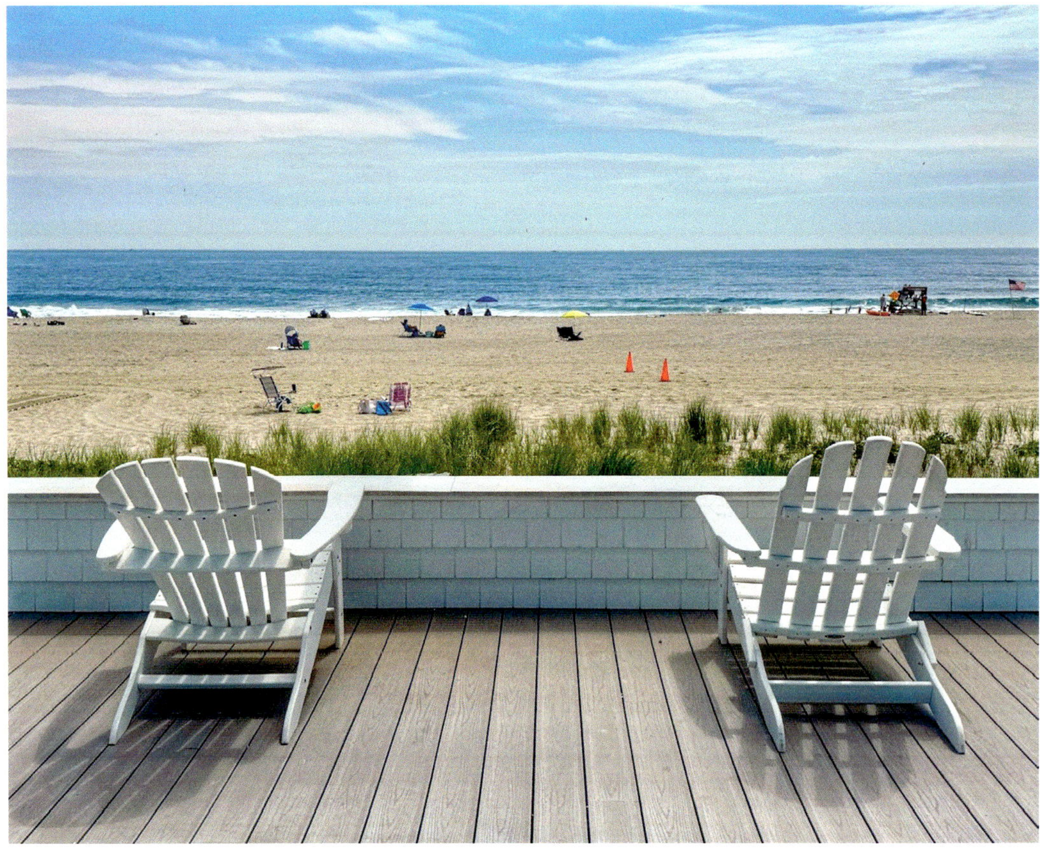

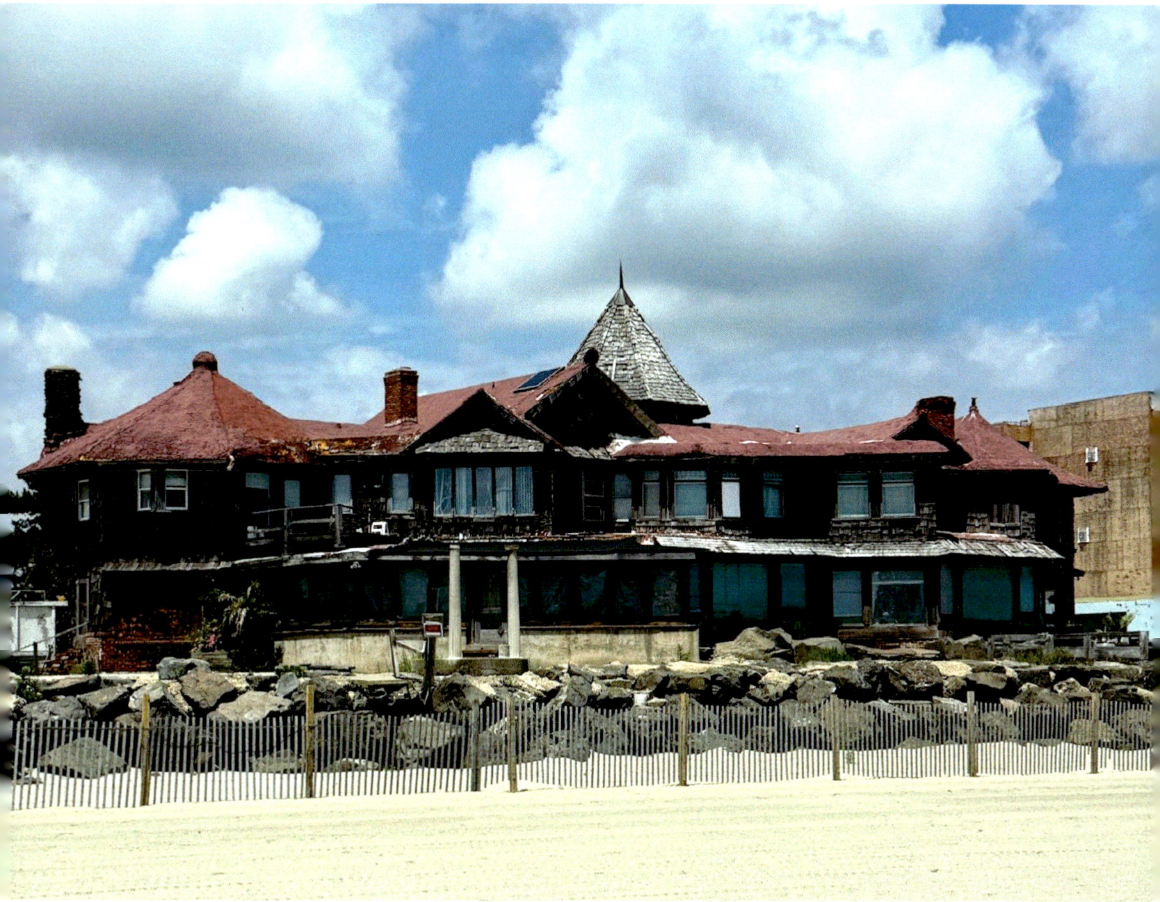

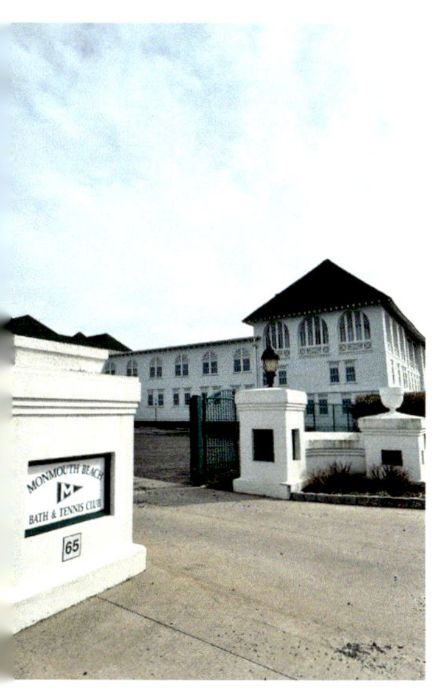

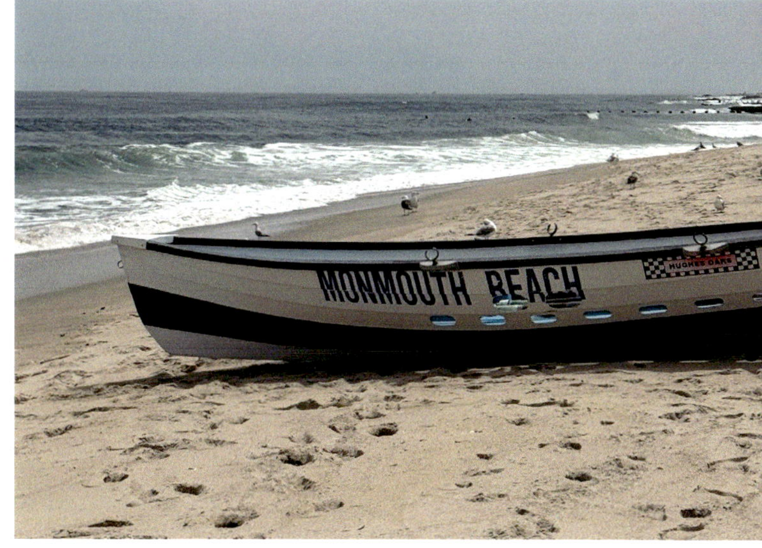
MONMOUTH BEACH

LONG BRANCH

Incorporated: 1867 (as *Long Branch Commission*)
Motto: "Tide In"
Origin of the name: Named for its location on the Long Branch of the South Shrewsbury River
Formed from: Portions of Ocean Township

As the local legend goes, original land patent holder John Slocum arrived in the Long Branch area around 1668. To resolve a land dispute, Slocum won a wrestling match with a local Lenape tribe member and was awarded 375 acres of land at a cost of £4. The Slocum family owned most of Long Branch for the next 200 years. In the first half of the 1800s, Long Branch was comprised mostly of farms, with a few large hotels. By the 1860s, it was already considered the "Monte Carlo" of America. During the summer of 1861, our country's newest first lady, Mary Todd Lincoln, vacationed here.

This started a trend of wealthy Americans vacationing in Long Branch, including the Vanderbilts and Goulds. Between the 1870s and the 1920s, the following seven presidents visited Long Branch: Grant, Hayes, Garfield, Arthur, Harrison, McKinley, and Wilson. In fact, James Garfield died here in 1881 from his assassination wounds. In honor of these visits, a beach on the north end of town was renamed "Seven Presidents Park," while St. James Chapel, in the Elberon section, was christened "the Church of the Presidents."

Featuring prominently in Long Branch over the years are its historic piers, which stretched out stoically over the ocean. There were five in total: The first, known as the "Bath House Pier," was built in 1828; the last, known as the "Amusement/Fishing Pier," was constructed in 1910. Sadly, this pier was damaged beyond repair in June 1987, when a horrific fire started in the Haunted Mansion and spread due to high winds. The charred skeleton of the abandoned pier remained until 1998, when it was finally dismantled. In 2005, Pier Village's shops and restaurants opened in the area where the piers once met the sand. Plans for a sixth pier in the area are currently being discussed, with a possible opening in 2025.

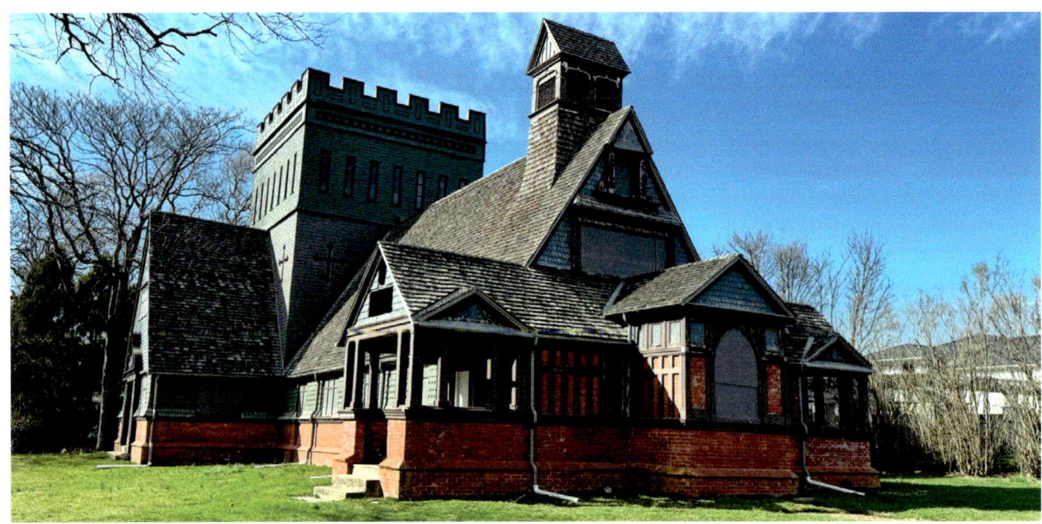

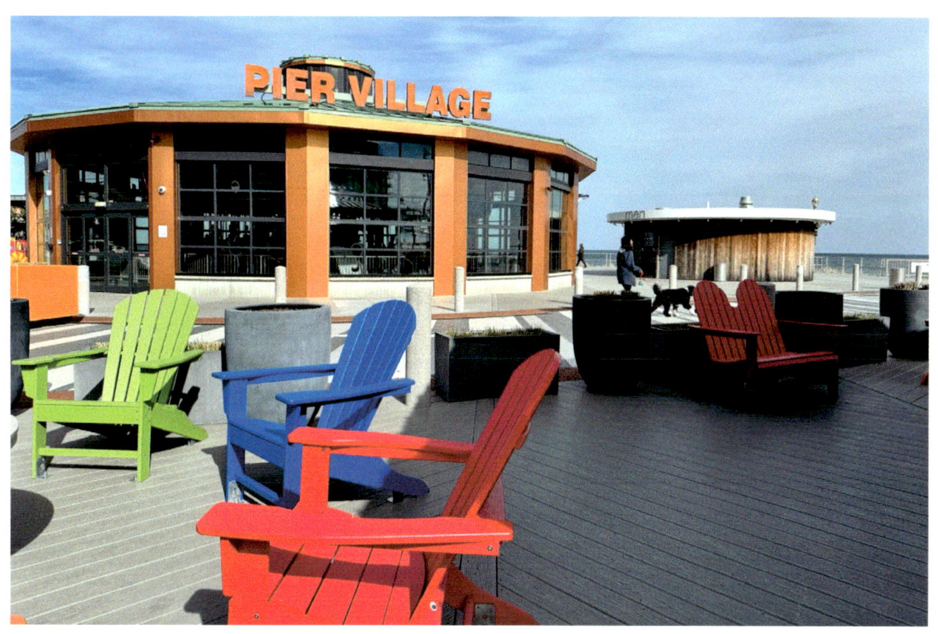
PIER VILLAGE
men

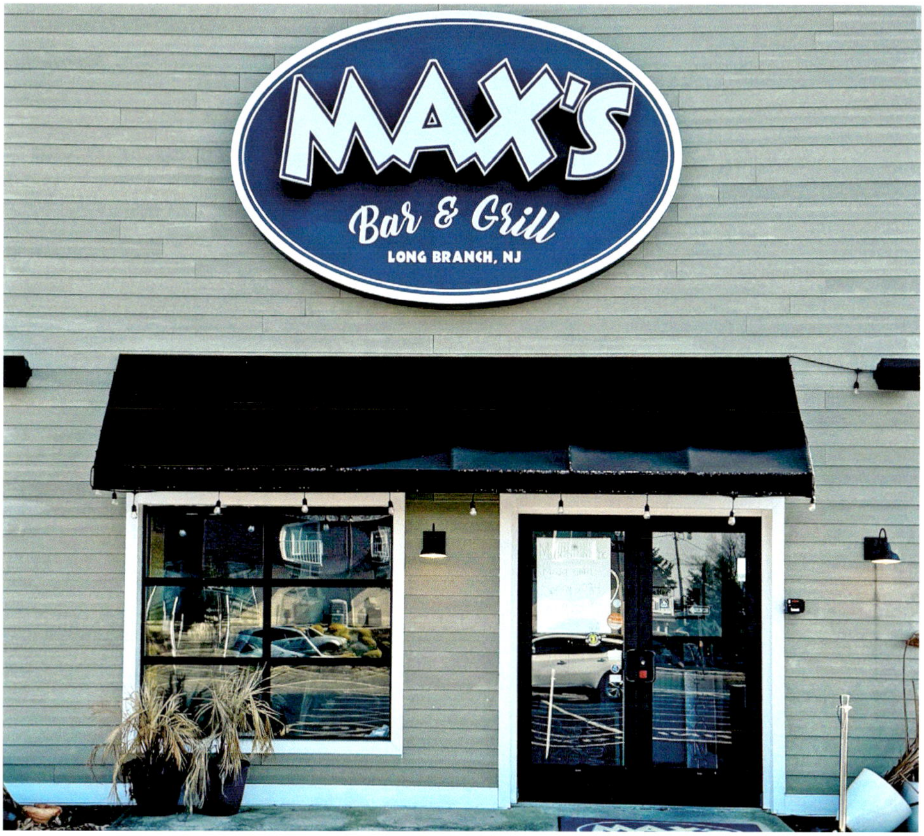

MAX'S
Bar & Grill
LONG BRANCH, NJ

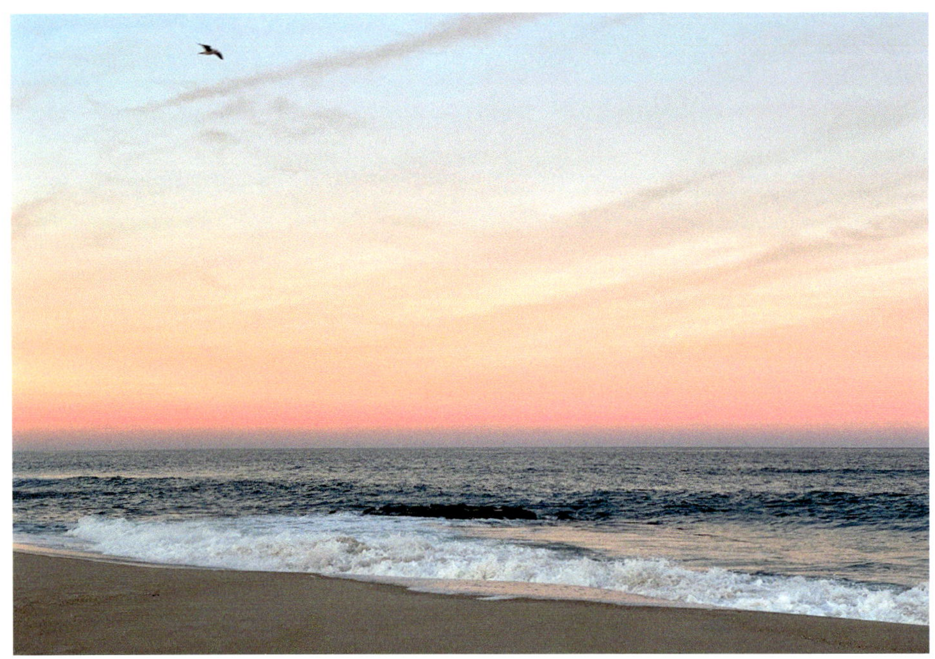

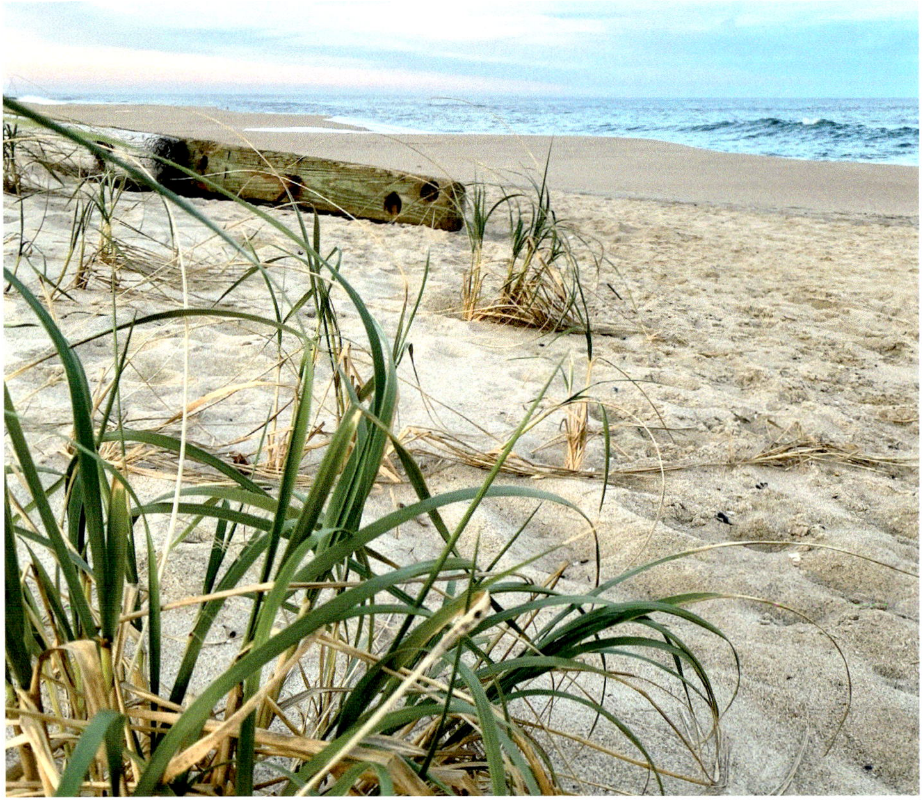

DEAL

Incorporated: 1898
Motto: None
Origin of the name: Named after the coastal town of Deal in Kent, England
Formed from: Portions of Ocean Township

In 1700, the "Long Branch and Deal Turnpike" was laid out along present-day Norwood Ave/Route 71, but it would be another 200 years before the area was developed into a resort community. During the Gilded Age, several grand mansions were built throughout the town, especially along the beach. Famous homeowners over the years include Jersey City Mayor Frank Hague and Mrs. Bruce Springsteen herself, Patti Scialfa. Although Deal only boasts 900 residents throughout its 1.2 miles of land, it was ranked as the second most expensive ZIP code in the state in 2024.

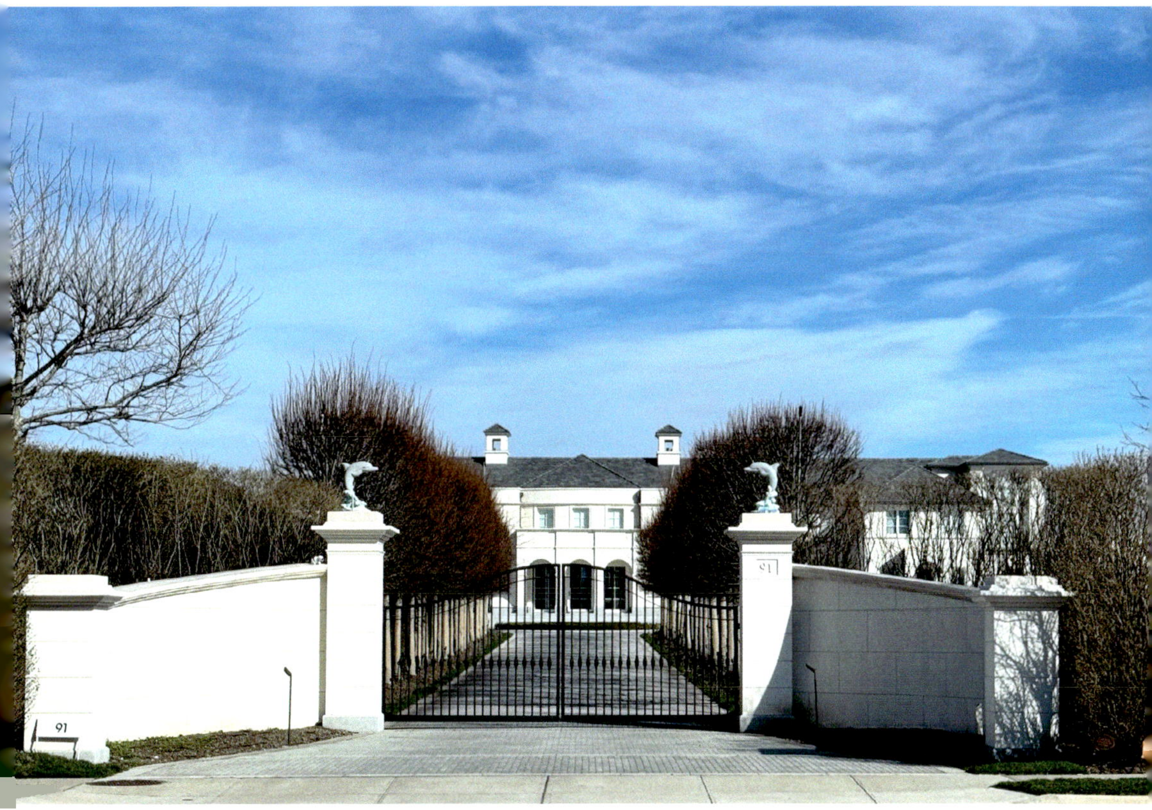

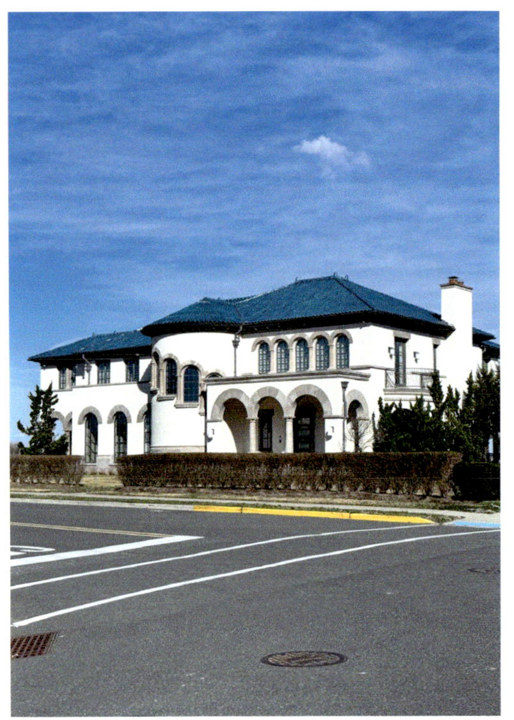

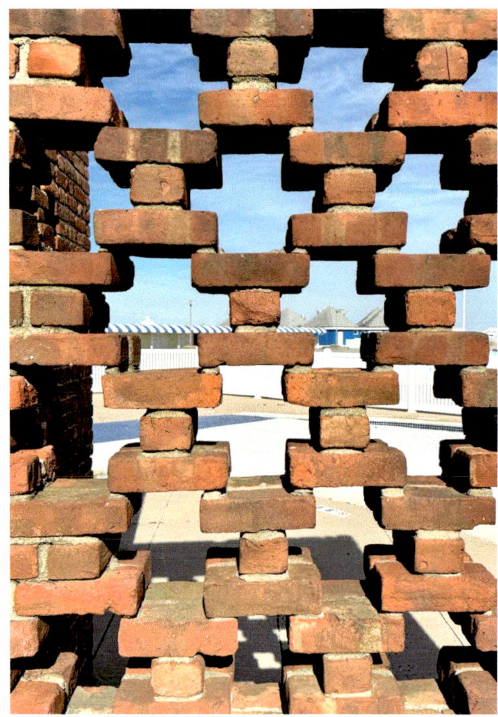

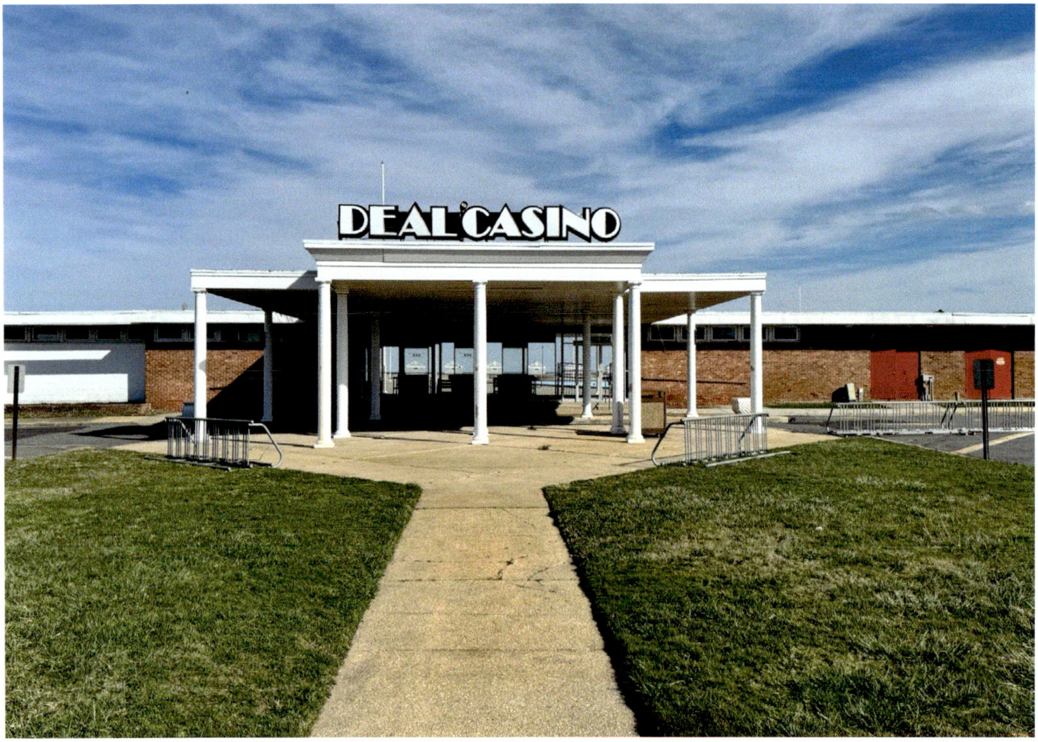

ALLENHURST

Incorporated: 1897
Motto: None
Origin of the name: Named for Abner Allen, one of the original settlers of the area
Formed from: Portions of Ocean Township

Another in a string of small, wealthy towns along the Monmouth County coast, Allenhurst is only five blocks long from north to south and has less than 500 residents. It was originally the farm of Abner Allen, the first settler in town. In 1854, the clipper ship *New Era* left Germany for New York but ran aground just off the coast of Asbury Park. Although 240 German immigrants lost their lives in the wreck, it could have been worse if not for the heroic efforts of the nearby lifesaving station keeper, Abner Allen, the first to respond. Like its neighboring towns to the north and south, Allenhurst became a prominent resort in the late 1800s once the railroad gave vacationers access to the area. The Allenhurst Beach Club, opened in the 1930s, has a half-million-gallon pool that fills up with fresh sea water every night during the summer. The Beach Club also oversees the eighty-year tradition of dying the ocean green on Labor Day weekend, to mark the end of the summer season.

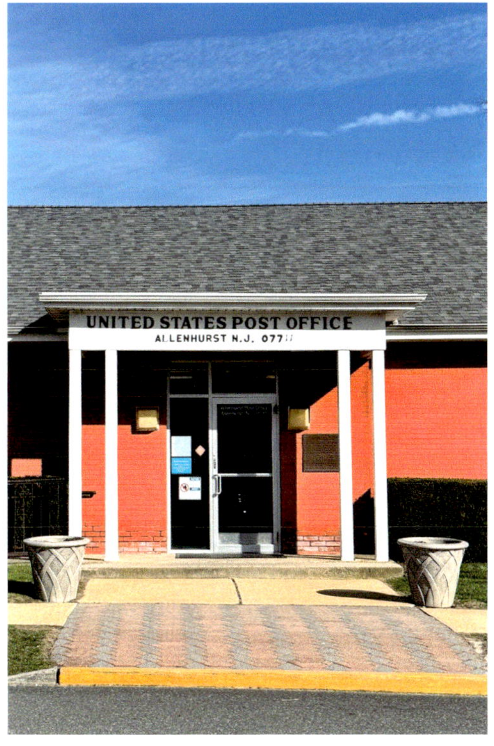

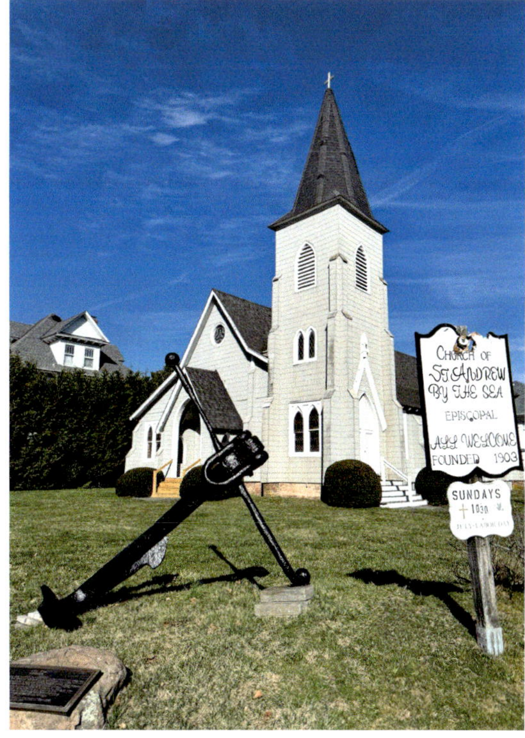

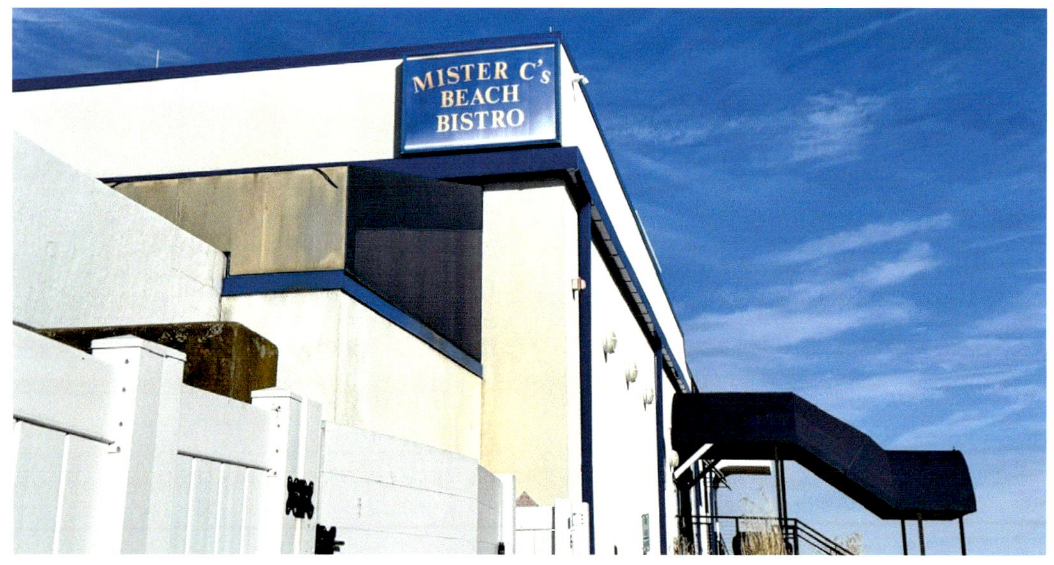
MISTER C's
BEACH
BISTRO

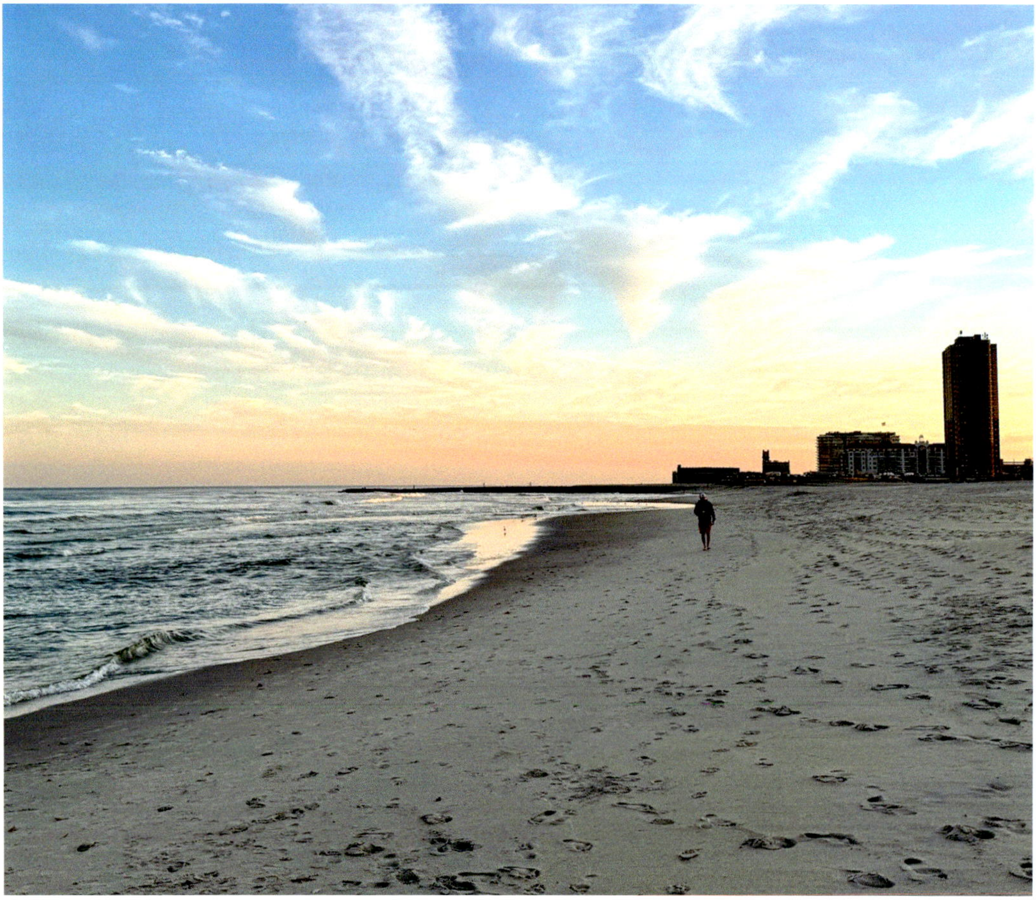

LOCH ARBOUR

Incorporated: 1957
Motto: None
Origin of the name: Lochaber, Scotland
Formed from: Portions of Ocean Township

Just like the towns of Sea Bright, Long Branch, Monmouth Beach, Deal, and Allenhurst, Loch Arbour "seceded" from Ocean Township in 1957, when plans for oceanfront condominiums were raised. Those against the overdevelopment of the area won and formed New Jersey's third smallest (and newest) community known as the Village of Loch Arbour, which is only two blocks wide and five blocks long. After Loch Arbour seceded, Ocean Township was left landlocked.

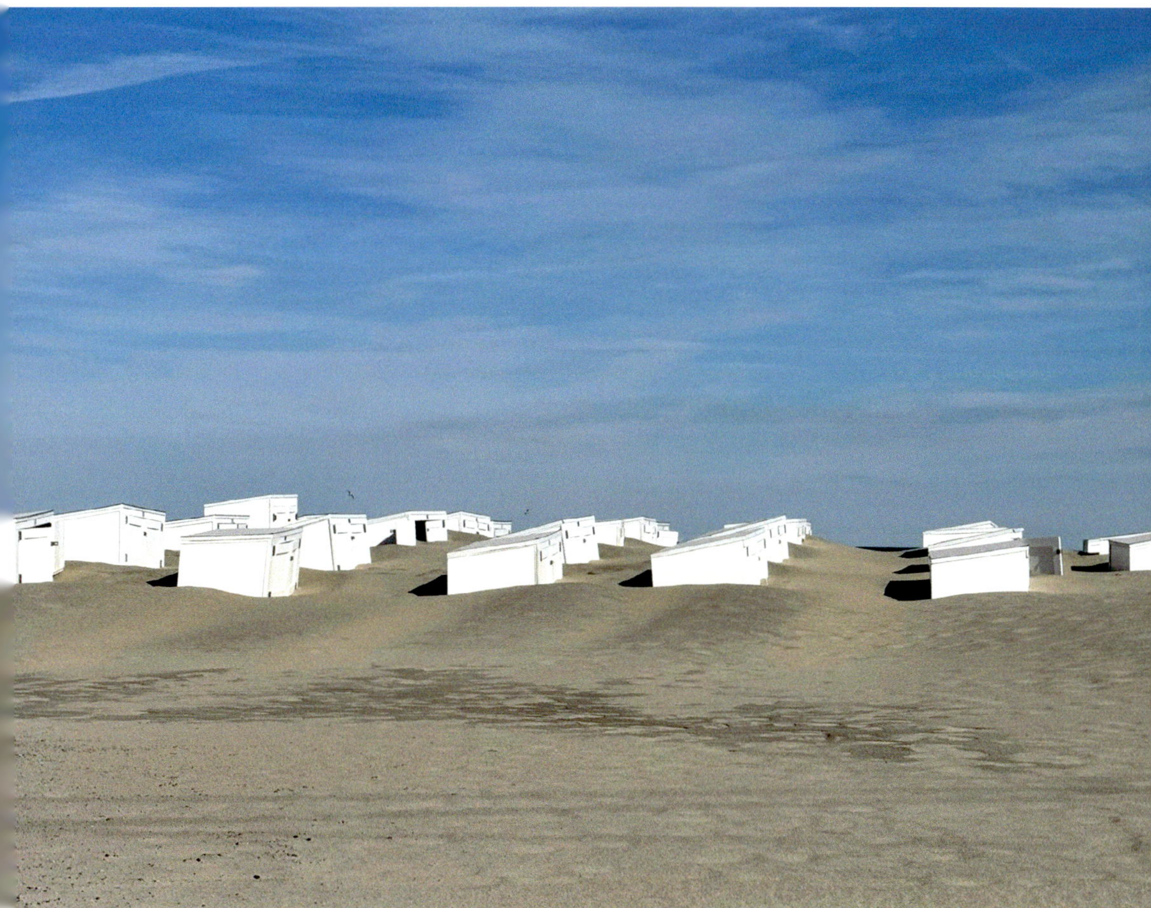

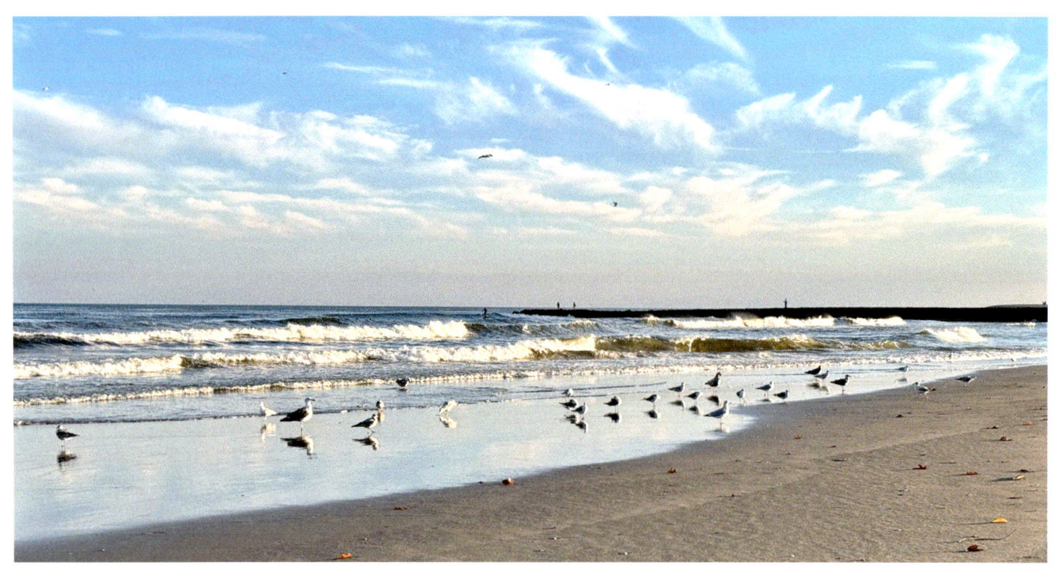

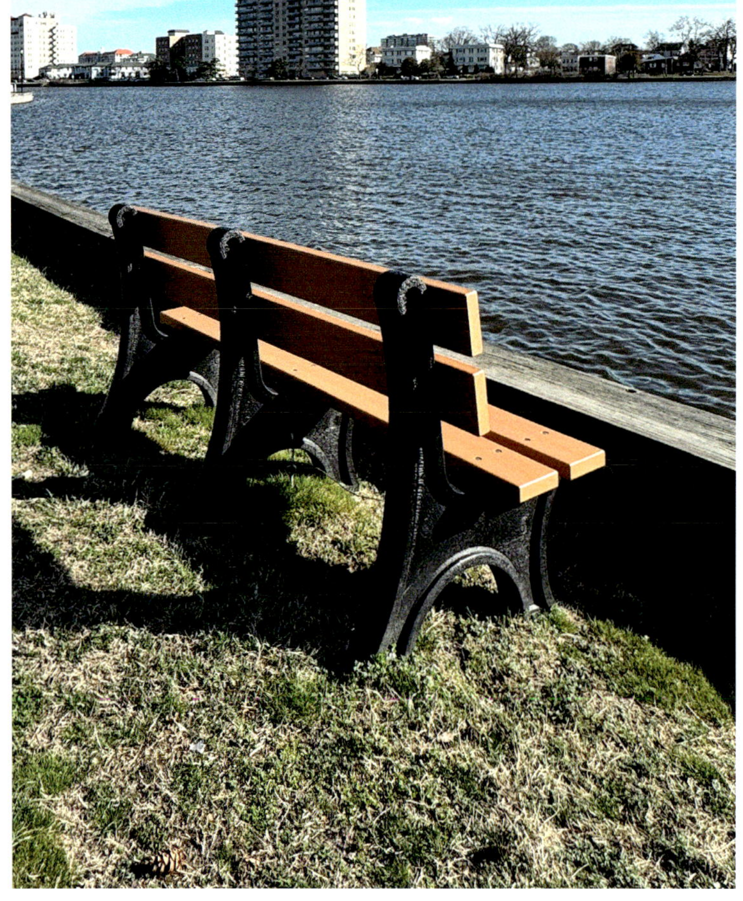

ASBURY PARK

Incorporated: 1874
Motto: "Stronger Than The Storm" and "Greetings from Asbury Park"
Origin of the name: Named for Francis Asbury, the first American bishop of the Methodist Episcopal Church in the United States
Formed from: Portions of Ocean Township

New Jersey State Senator, brush manufacturer, and real estate developer James Bradley conceived of Asbury Park in 1871. He was close with the founders of the neighboring Methodist retreat in Ocean Grove and planned to develop the land just to the north. As a tribute, he named the new resort Asbury Park, after Bishop Francis Asbury, the founder of Methodism in the United States. Bradley installed a boardwalk, a pier and electrical lighting by the beach, which led to other attractions such as Palace Amusements, home of the original "Tillie" in 1888 (demolished in 2004).

The addition of the Paramount Theatre, Convention Hall, and Carousel House in the 1920s, followed by the wreck of the SS *Morro Castle* just yards offshore in 1934, led to a boom in tourism in Asbury. The city saw its first decline in the early 1950s with the opening of the Garden State Parkway, which allowed tourists to easily reach resort towns further south.

Throughout the '60s, '70s, and '80s, musicians flocked to Asbury Park to play in the clubs along Cookman Avenue like the Upstage Club, the Stone Pony on Ocean Avenue, as well as the bigger theaters like the Paramount and Convention Hall. Artists such as Stevie Wonder, the Beach Boys, the Doors, Black Sabbath, The Ramones, Slayer, Stone Temple Pilots, and Green Day all entertained fans at Asbury. And of course Bruce Springsteen and Bon Jovi.

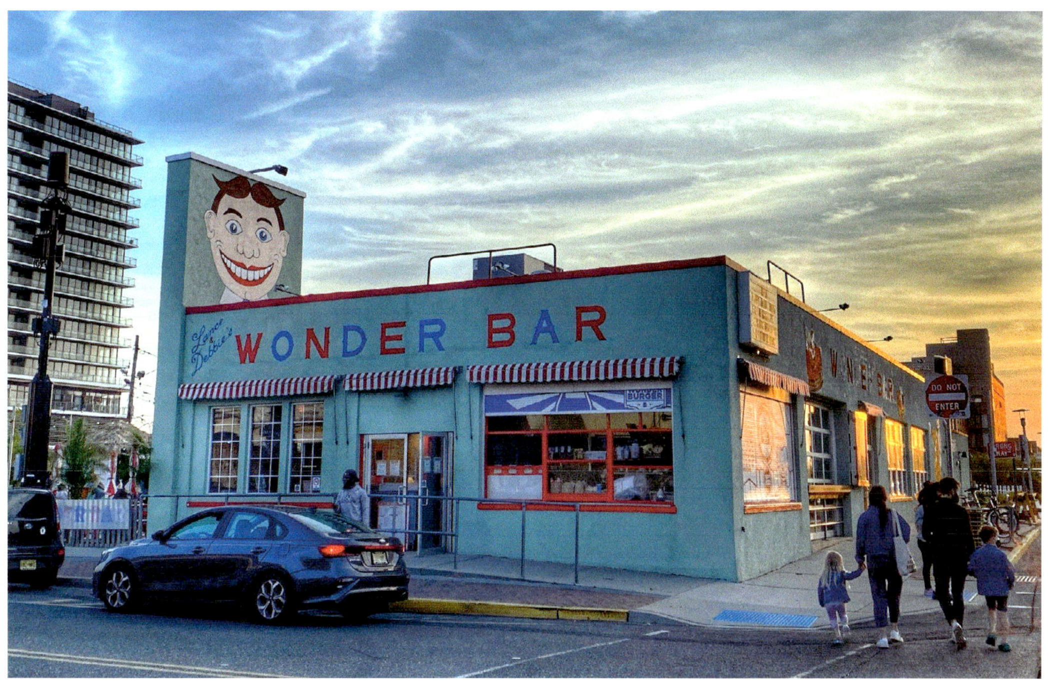

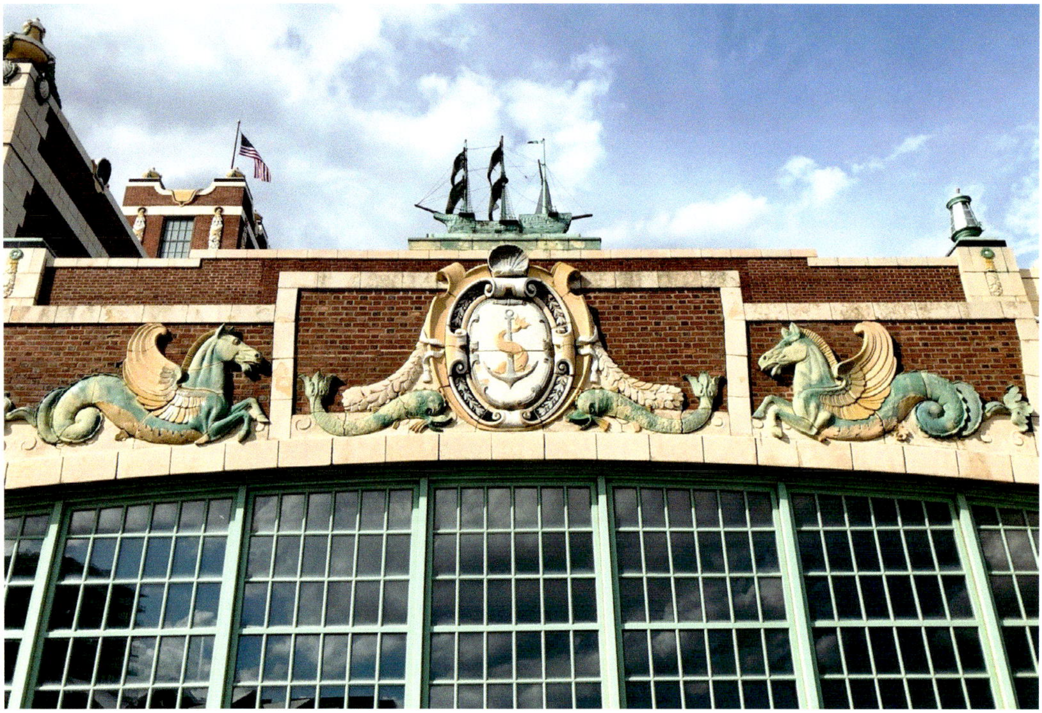

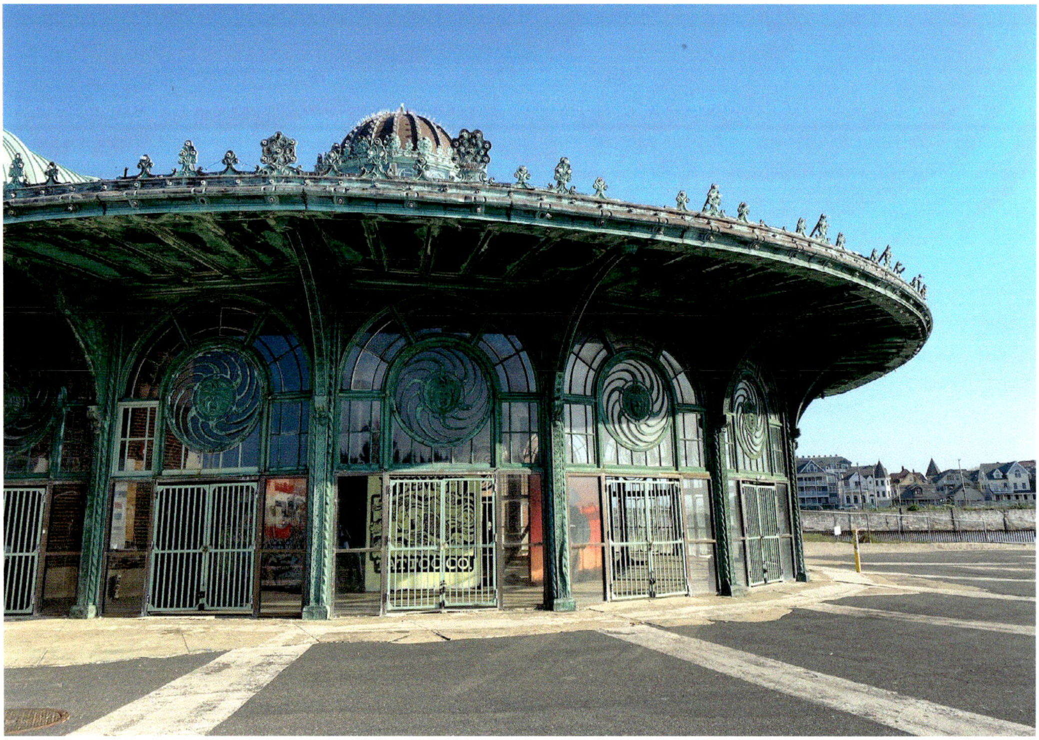

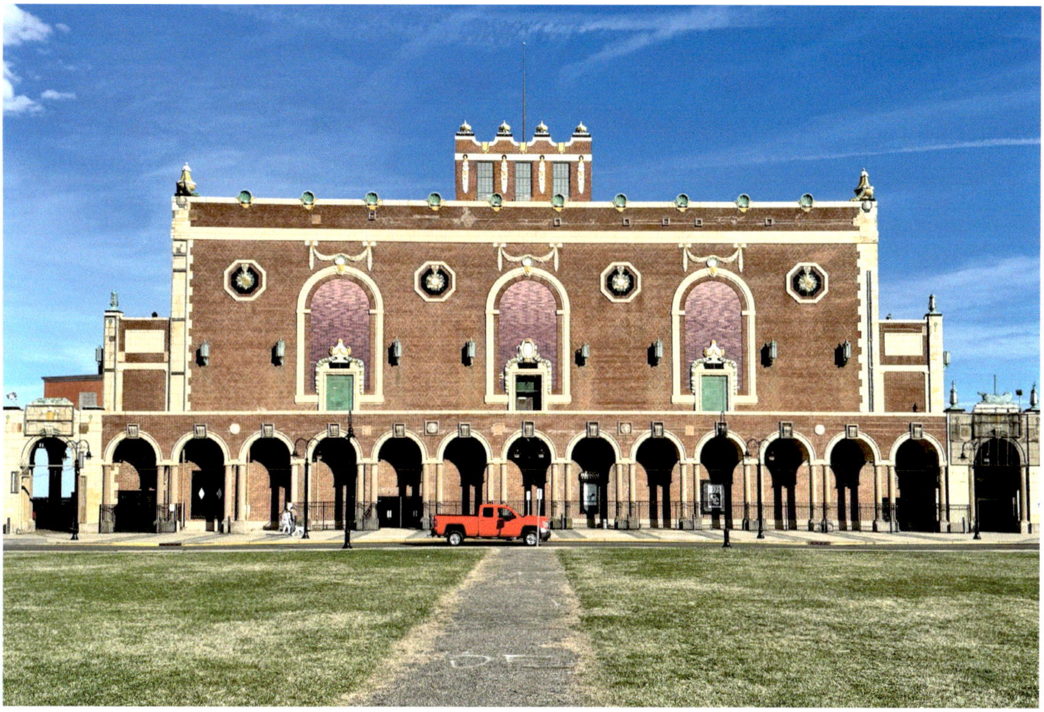

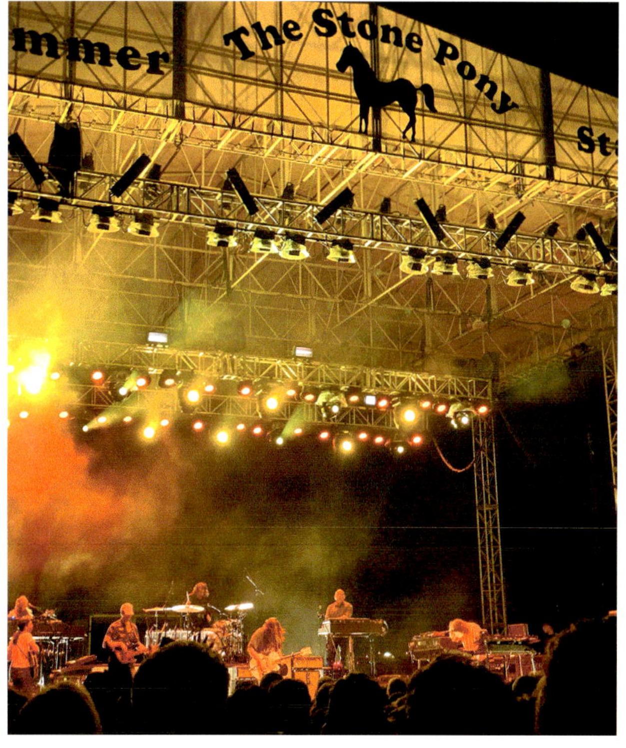
mmer
The Stone Pony
St

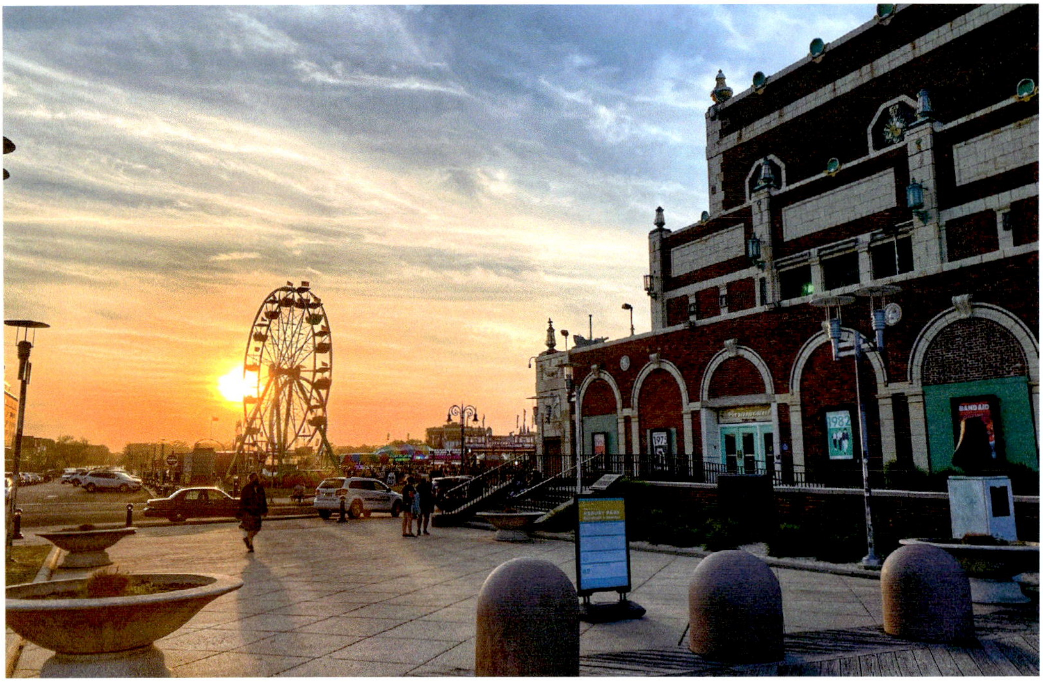

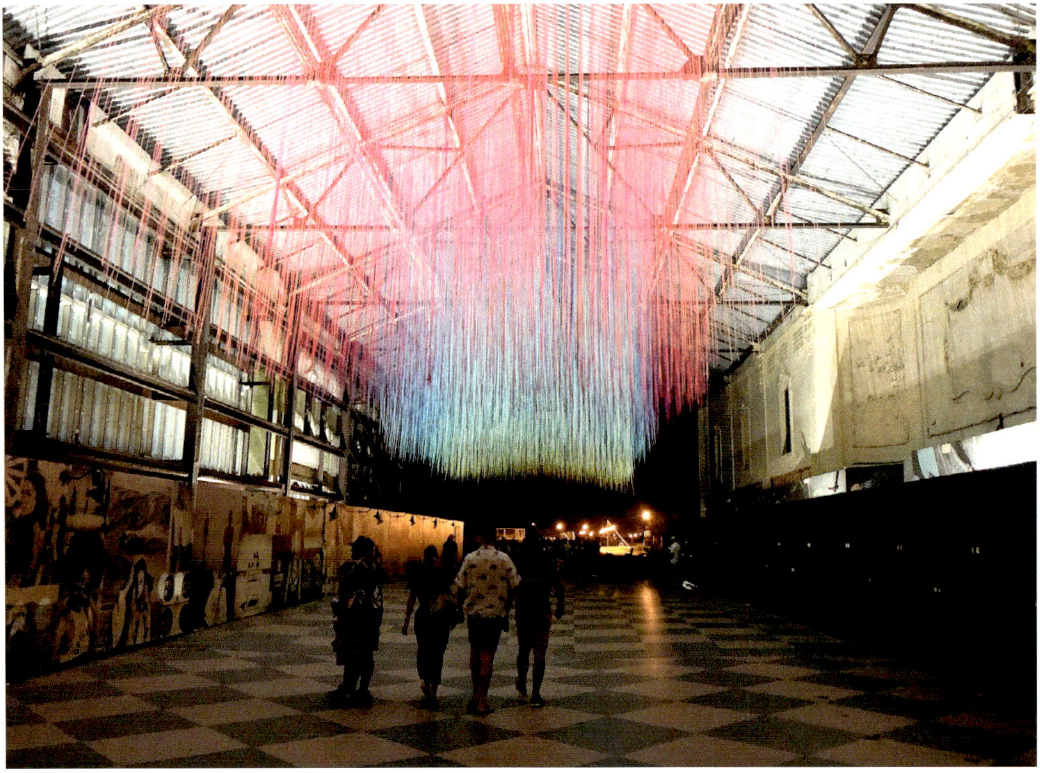

OCEAN GROVE (NEPTUNE TOWNSHIP)

Incorporated: 1870, as the Ocean Grove Camp Meeting Association
Motto: "God's Square Mile at the Jersey Shore"
Origin of the name: The Association set up their retreat in a grove of trees
Formed from: Portions of Ocean Township

Methodist ministers were searching for a home in New Jersey where "recreation and religion went hand in hand." After an exhaustive search, they stumbled upon a peaceful grove of trees in 1869, surrounded by lakes and the Atlantic Ocean, and free of mosquitoes. The ministers set up their camp starting with twenty tents, and lots were leased to worshipers, who were expected to refrain from alcohol, tobacco, chewing gum, playing cards, and reading fiction. In fact, until Ocean Grove was folded into Neptune Township in 1981, it had its own unique set of laws, including no horses, wagons or cars allowed to be driven on Sundays.

The wooden Great Auditorium was constructed in 1894, and became the centerpiece of the town, hosting a variety of speakers, performances, and concerts over the years, including John Philip Sousa, Tony Bennett, and Ray Charles. Surrounding the auditorium are 114 tents, which are used from May to September, a tradition which started in 1869. Each tent is connected to a "shed," which houses a kitchen and bathroom. There is a ten-year wait for a tent rental.

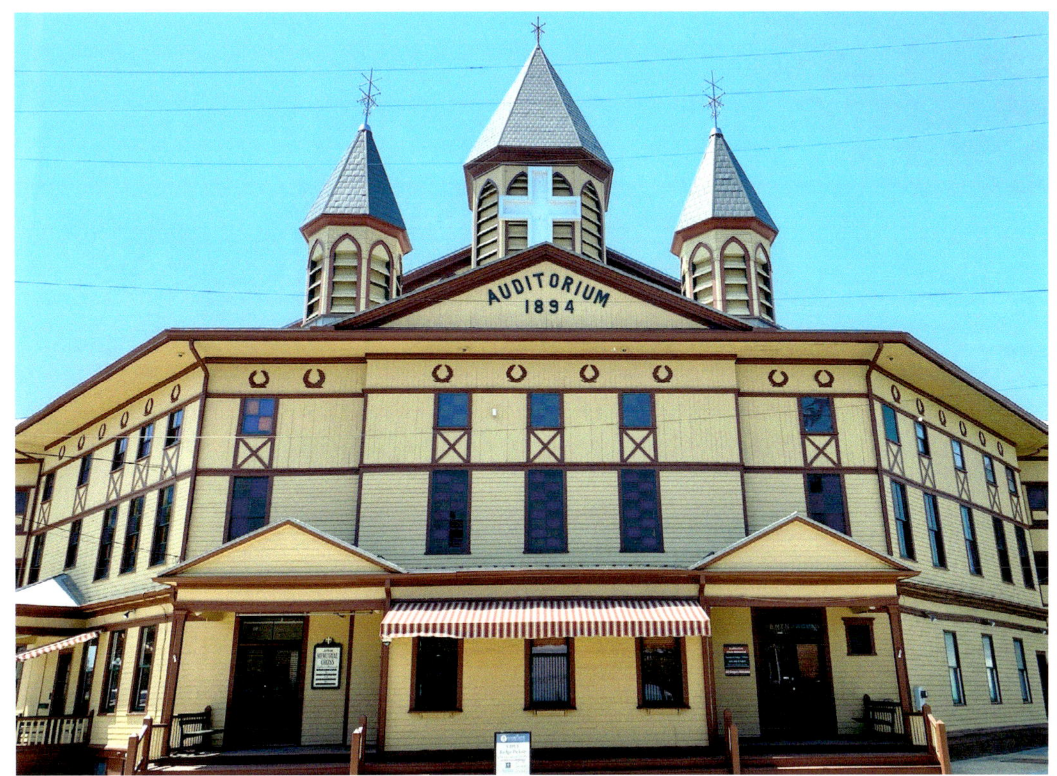

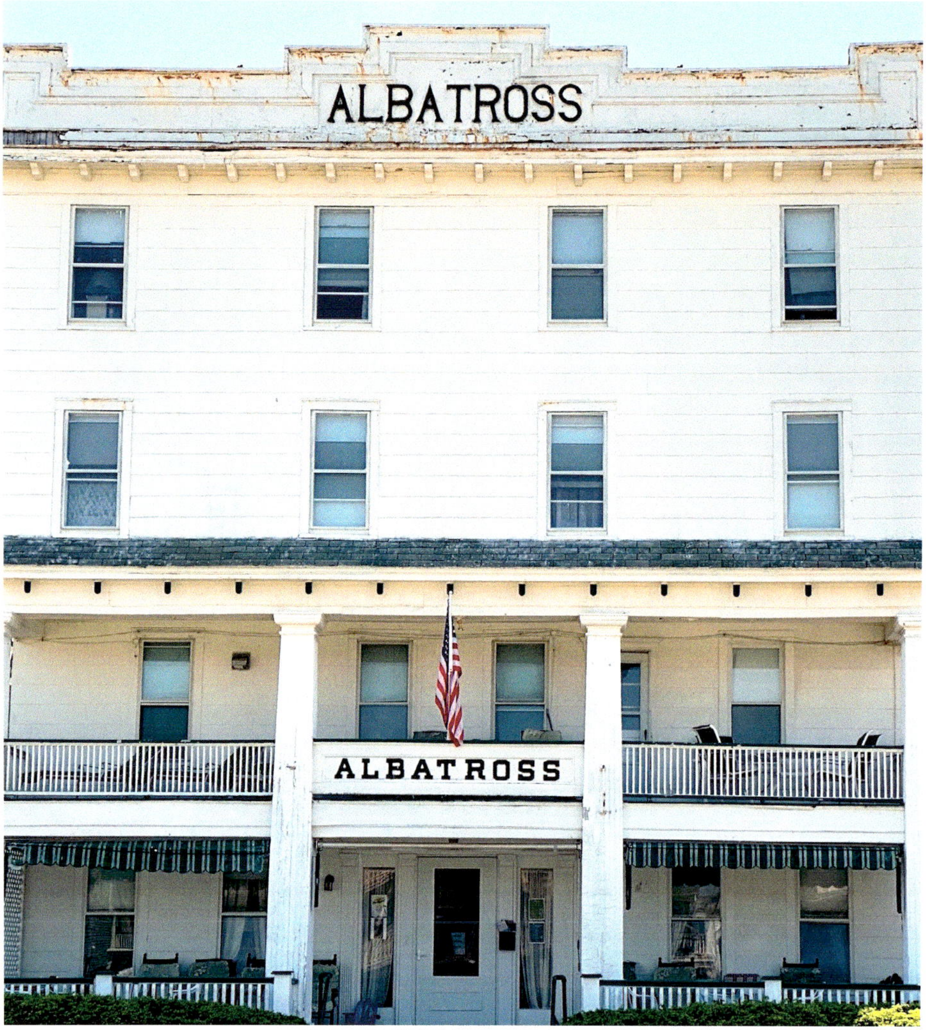

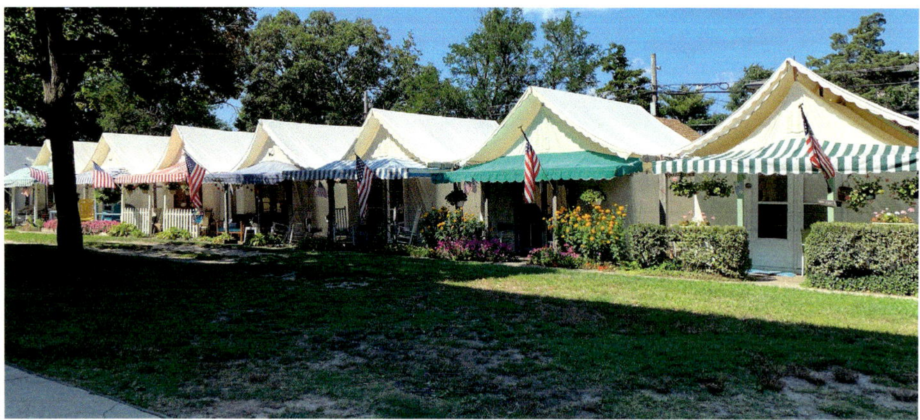

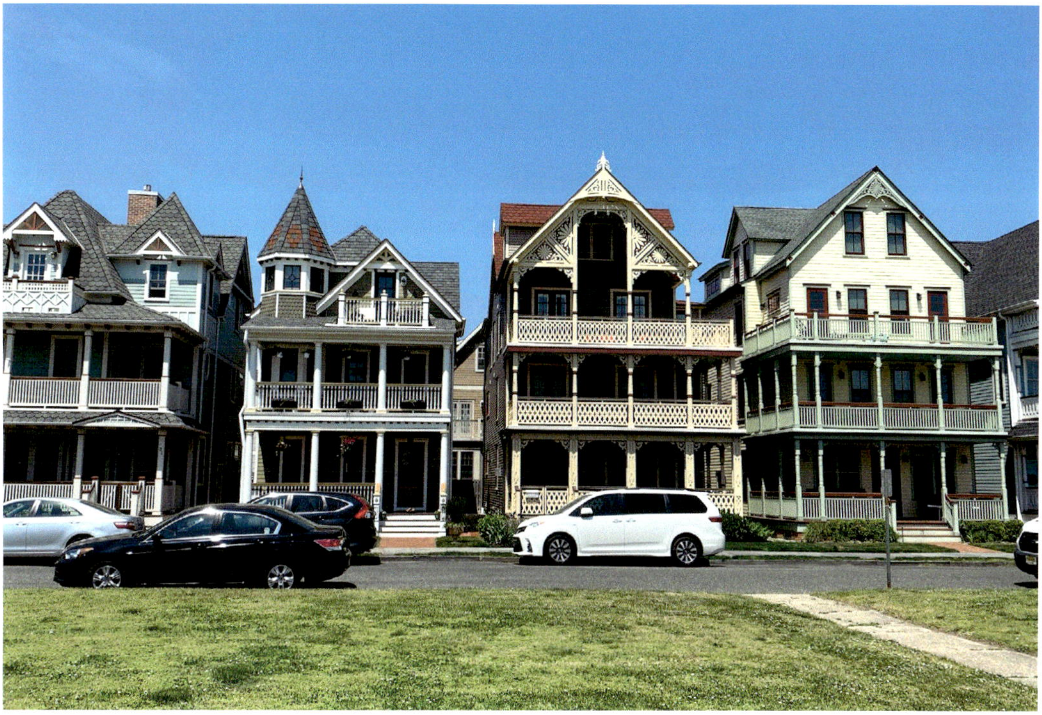

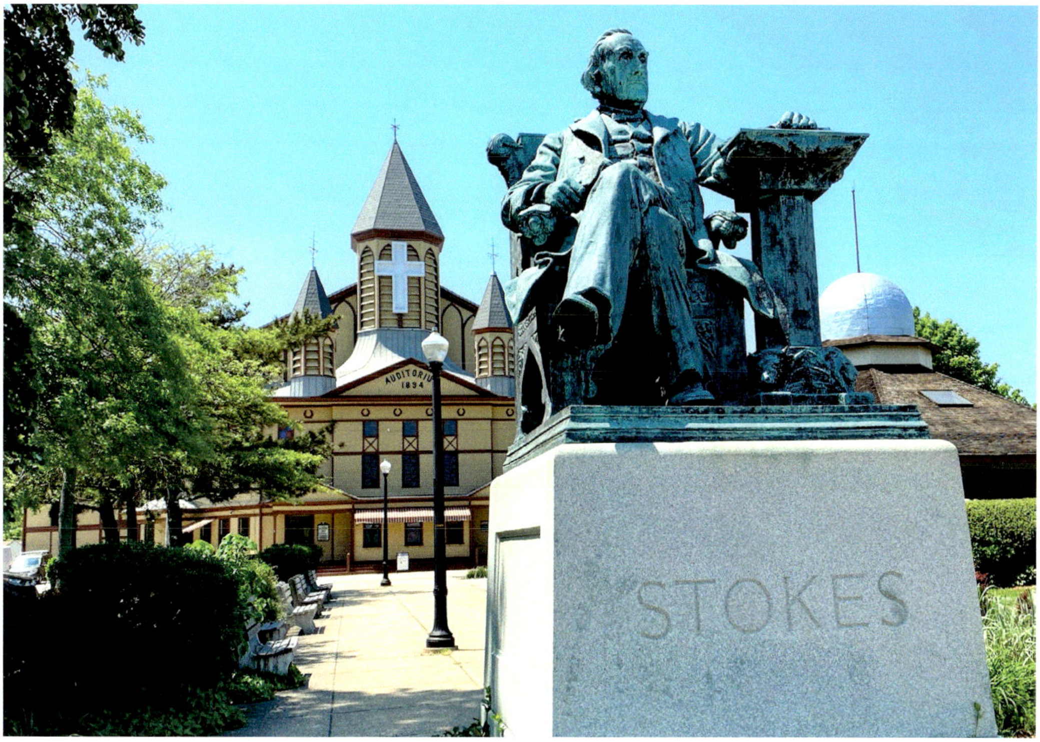

BRADLEY BEACH

Incorporated:	1893
Motto:	"New Jersey's Family Resort"
Origin of the name:	Named after James Bradley, land investor and founder of Asbury Park
Formed from:	Portions of Ocean Township & Neptune Township
Previous Names:	Ocean Park

Legend has it that notorious pirate Captain William Kidd anchored off Sylvan Lake in 1679 and buried his famed treasure around Brinley Avenue. Nearly two centuries later, land investors Willian Bradner and James Bradley (the founder of Asbury Park) acquired 54 acres of land between Avon-by-The-Sea and Ocean Grove in 1871. They originally called their land Ocean Park but were soon informed by the post office that the name was too close to nearby Ocean Port, so they changed it to Bradley Beach. By 1893, residents pushed forth a referendum to separate from Neptune Township, and the Borough of Bradley Beach was established. Bradley Beach was the first town to charge for beach access in 1929, when they began minting and selling their own tin badges. By the 1930s, Bradley Beach was a bustling shore community, boasting nearly a mile of shoreline, hundreds of dressing rooms, two large swimming pools, hot water baths, and numerous shoppes. Today, Bradley Beach flourishes as a quiet family resort town, with an active Main Street and peaceful boardwalk.

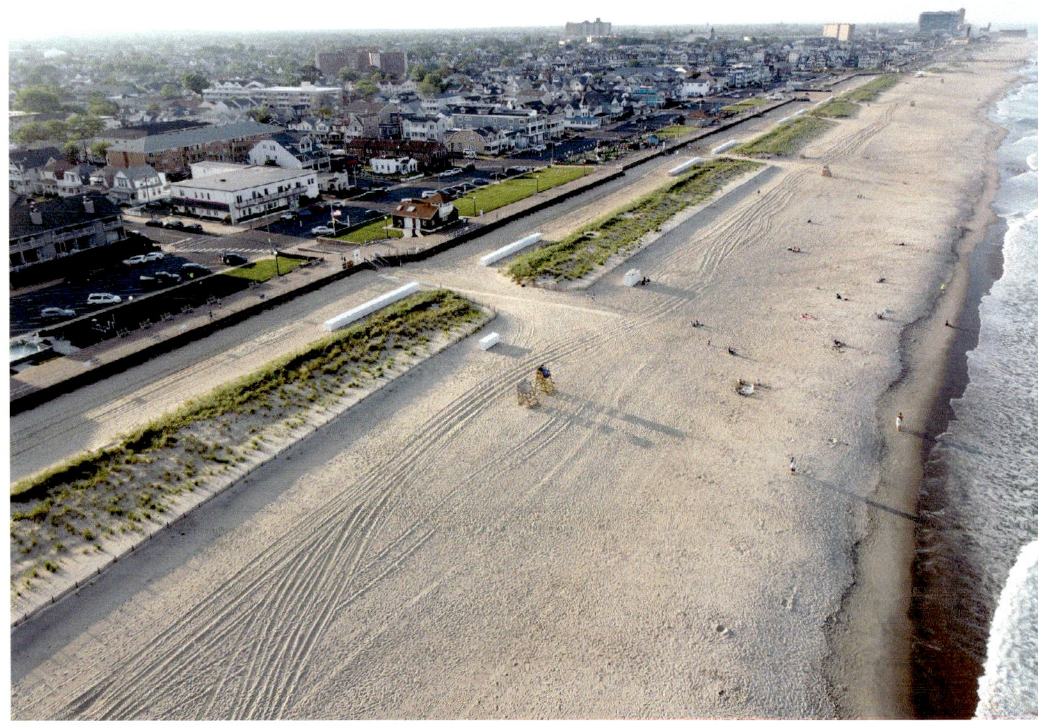

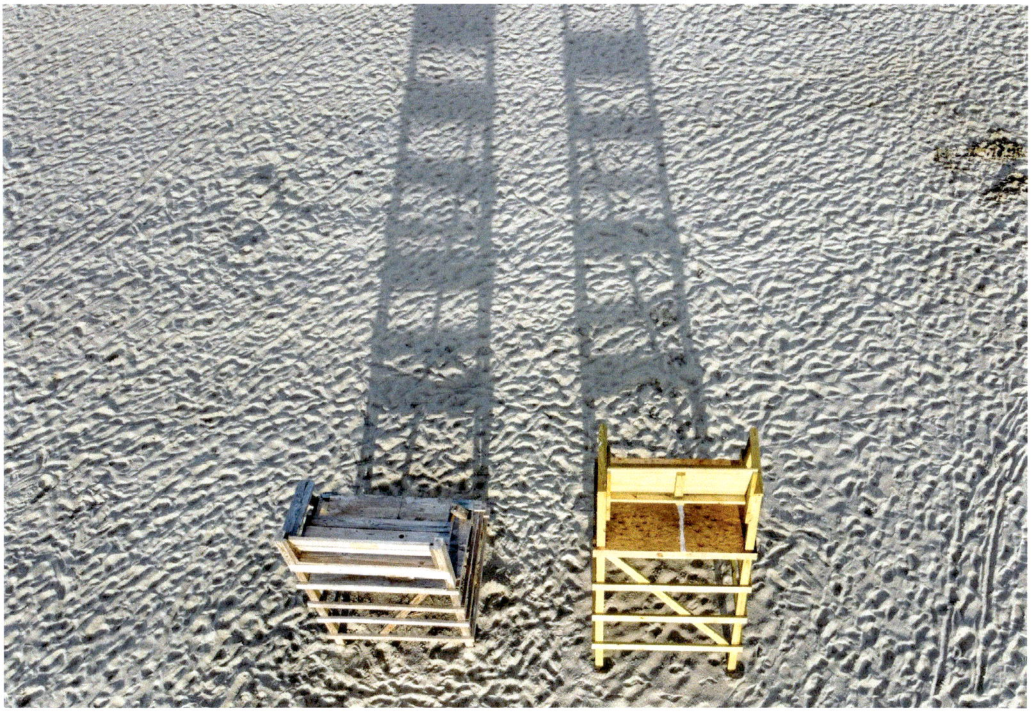

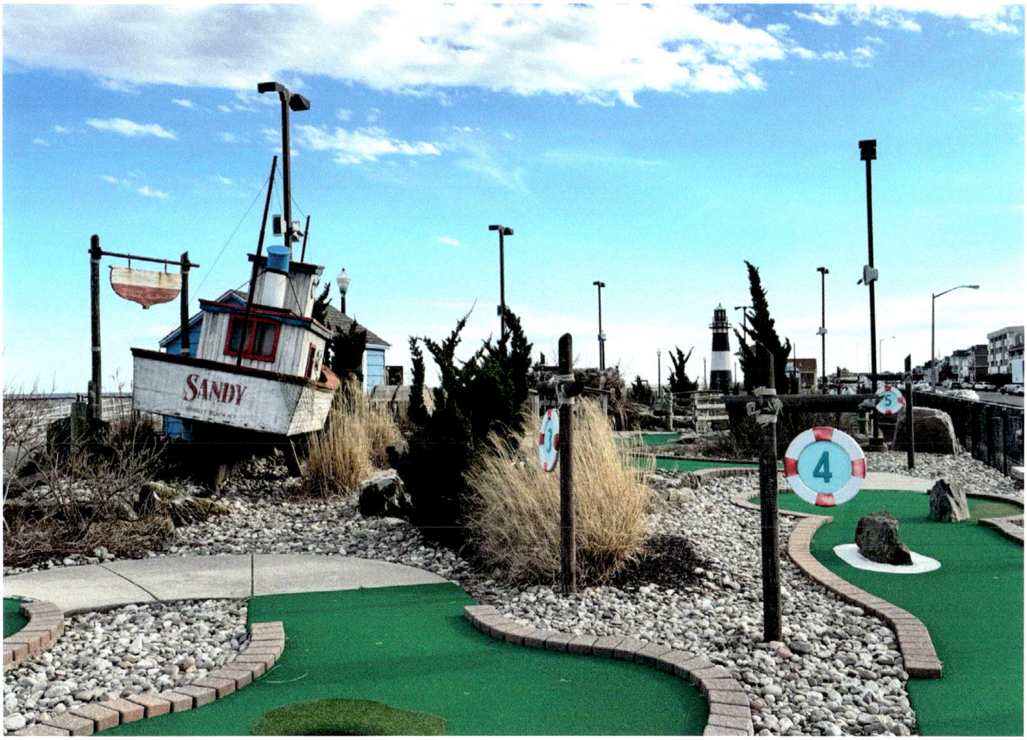

SANDY

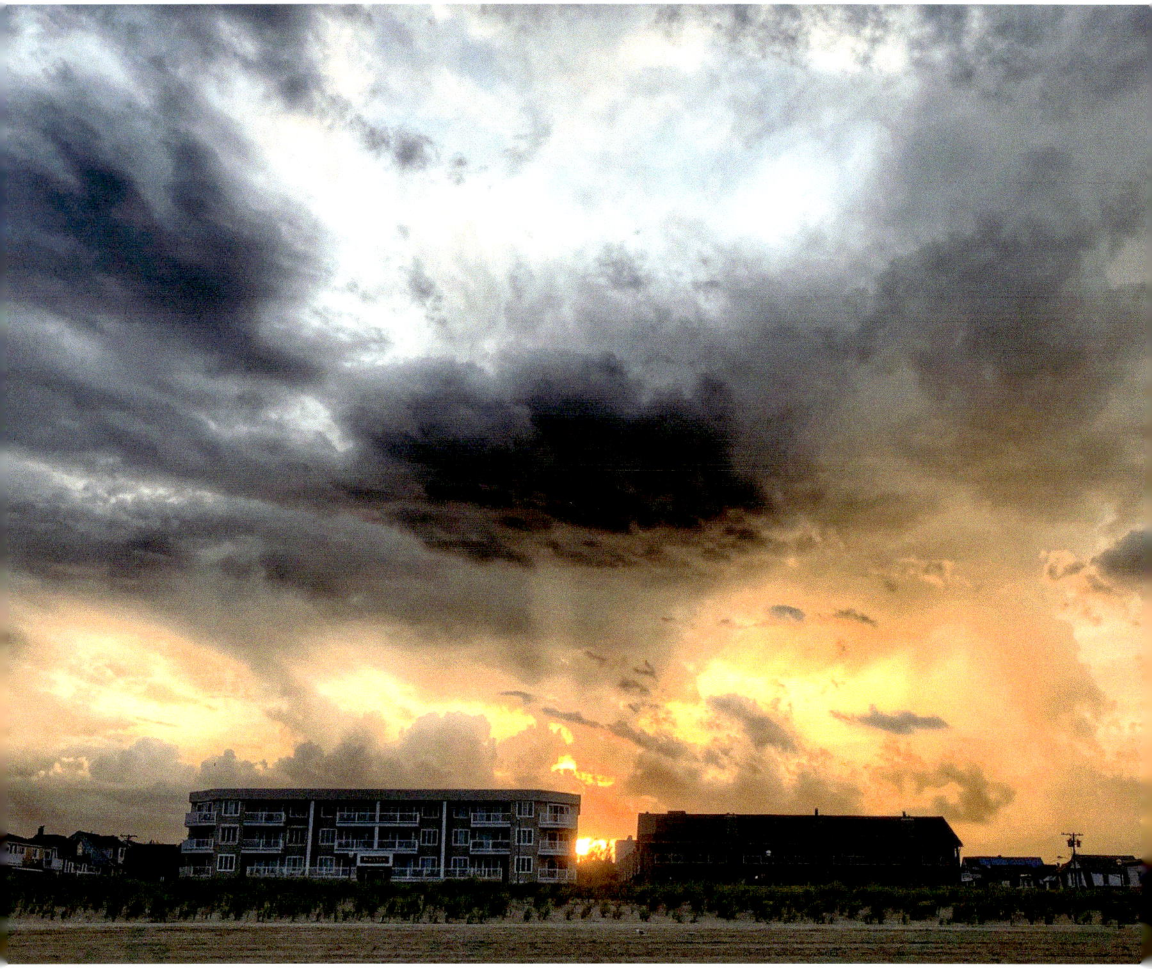

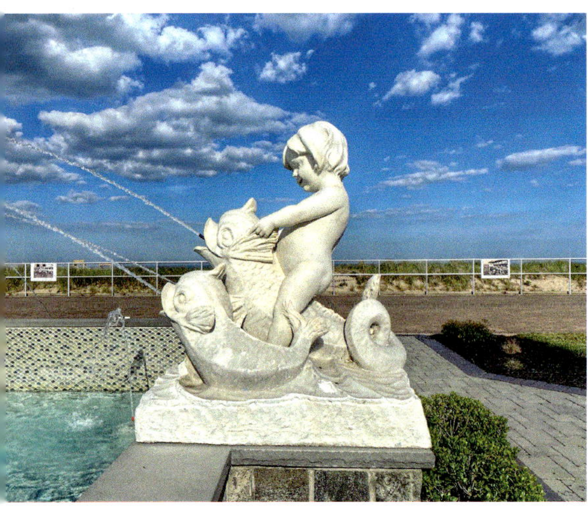

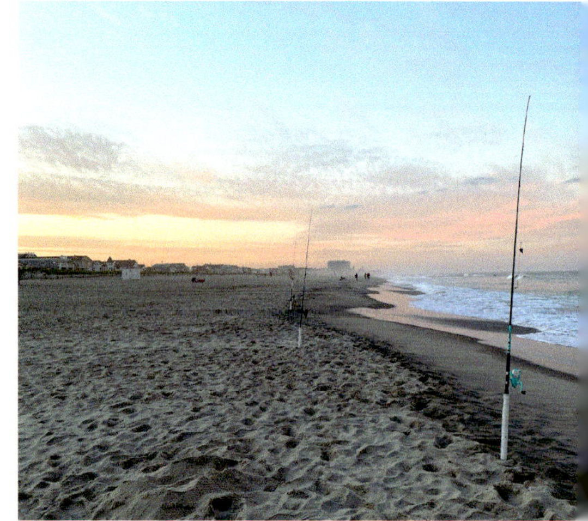

AVON-BY-THE-SEA

Incorporated: 1900
Motto: None
Origin of the name: Many theories, including being named for Avon, England, and after
                         Nels Avone, son of Norse explorer Lief Erikson, who is said to have
                         visited these shores in 1027
Formed from: Portions of Neptune City
Previous names: New Branch, Swanton Tract, Lewis Greene Property, Key East

Philadelphia tobacconist Edward Batchelor purchased 300 acres of land north of Shark River in 1878 as a potential relocation for his tobacco firm, but after the success of nearby Long Branch, Ocean Grove, and Asbury Park, decided to develop the town into a beachfront resort instead. Over the next ten years, Batchelor helped fund everything needed to install the proper infrastructure needed for the half-mile town, including roads, sewers, hotels, a boardwalk, and a beachfront pavilion. The Shark River Bridge was built in 1932 and connects Avon with Belmar via Ocean Avenue.

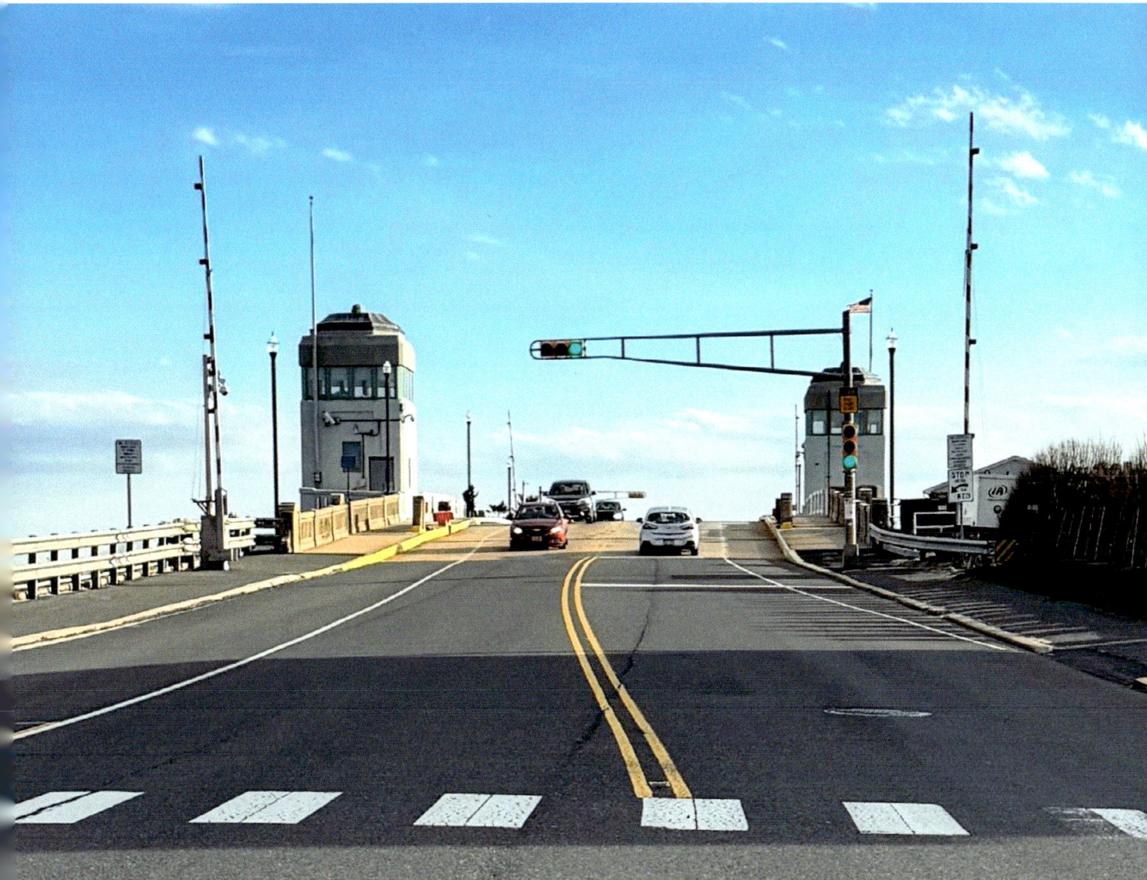

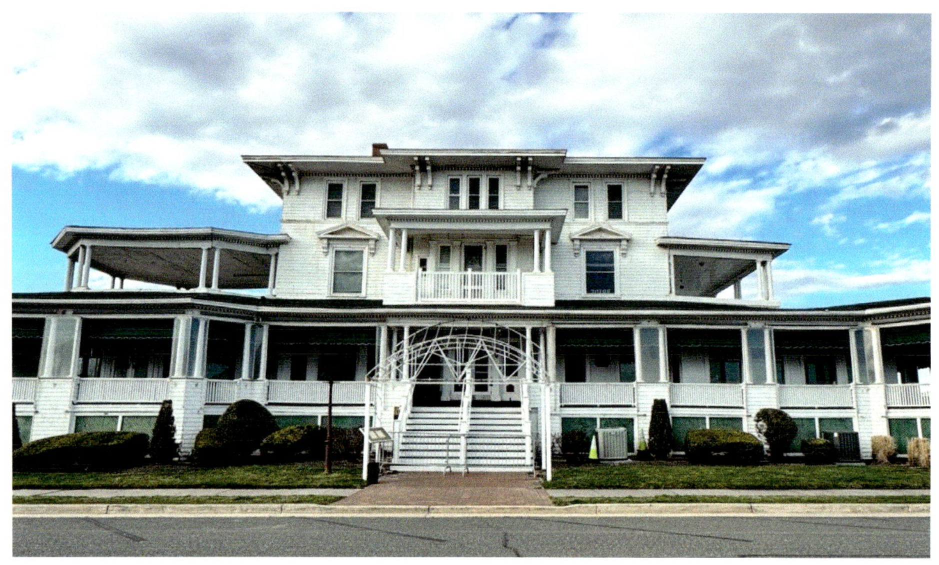

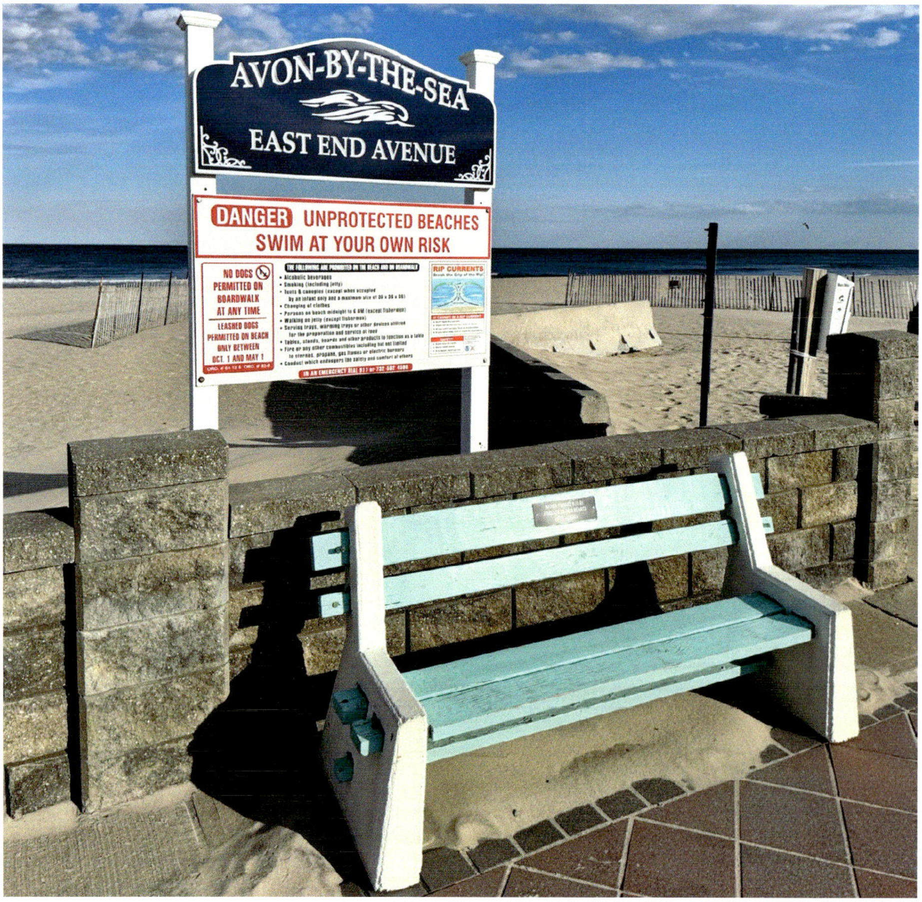

AVON-BY-THE-SEA
EAST END AVENUE
DANGER UNPROTECTED BEACHES
SWIM AT YOUR OWN RISK
NO DOGS
PERMITTED ON
BOARDWALK
AT ANY TIME
LEASHED DOGS
PERMITTED ON BEACH
ONLY BETWEEN
OCT. 1 AND MAY 1
RIP CURRENTS

BELMAR

Incorporated: 1885 (as Ocean Beach), 1889 (as Elcho), 1889 (as Belmar)
Motto: "Duty and Service"
Origin of the name: Belmar means "beautiful sea" in Italian
Formed from: Portions of Wall Township
Previous names: Ocean Beach, Elcho/Elko

"Exit 98" off the Garden State Parkway brings vacationers directly to Belmar (after an anticipatory ride eastward along Route 138). Long before these roads were constructed, this land was home to the Lenape people, who enjoyed the abundance of fish, crabs, oysters, clams, and waterfowl, as most of the land was surrounded by water (the Atlantic Ocean, Shark River, Lake Como, and Silver Lake). In 1872, the same religious group from nearby Ocean Grove planned a second community from the inlet to 12th Avenue and called it "Ocean Beach." The original design called for numbered east/west avenues and alphabetized north/south streets, which still exist today. Over the next few years, the community briefly changed its name to Elko, and then Belmar, and expanded southward to Spring Lake. Shoppers at 7-Eleven on 8th and Ocean Avenue can view the tall foremast of the SS *Malta,* a ship that ran aground only 100 yards offshore in 1885. A few blocks to the north stands the Belmar Fishing Club, a private pier built in 1909 in the Spanish mission style. By the middle of the twentieth century, Belmar had become a premier vacation spot, with dozens of restaurants and shops, pristine beaches, and great surfing. Over the years, Belmar residents and visitors have come to enjoy such notable establishments as Kleins Fish Market, D'Jais, and, more recently, Marina Grille and 9th Avenue Pier.

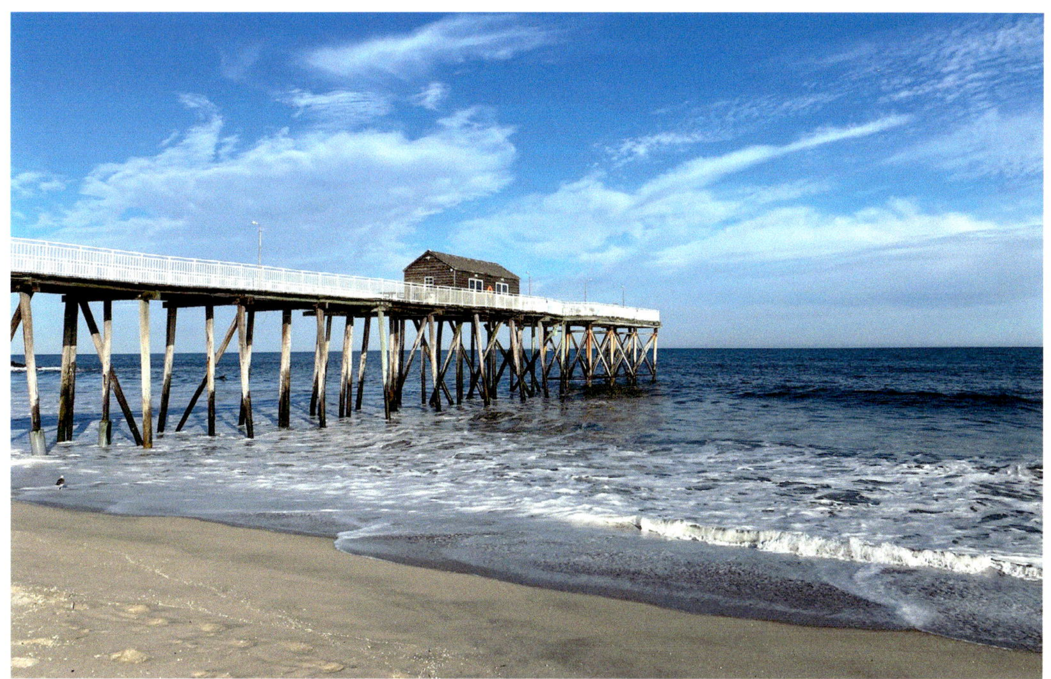

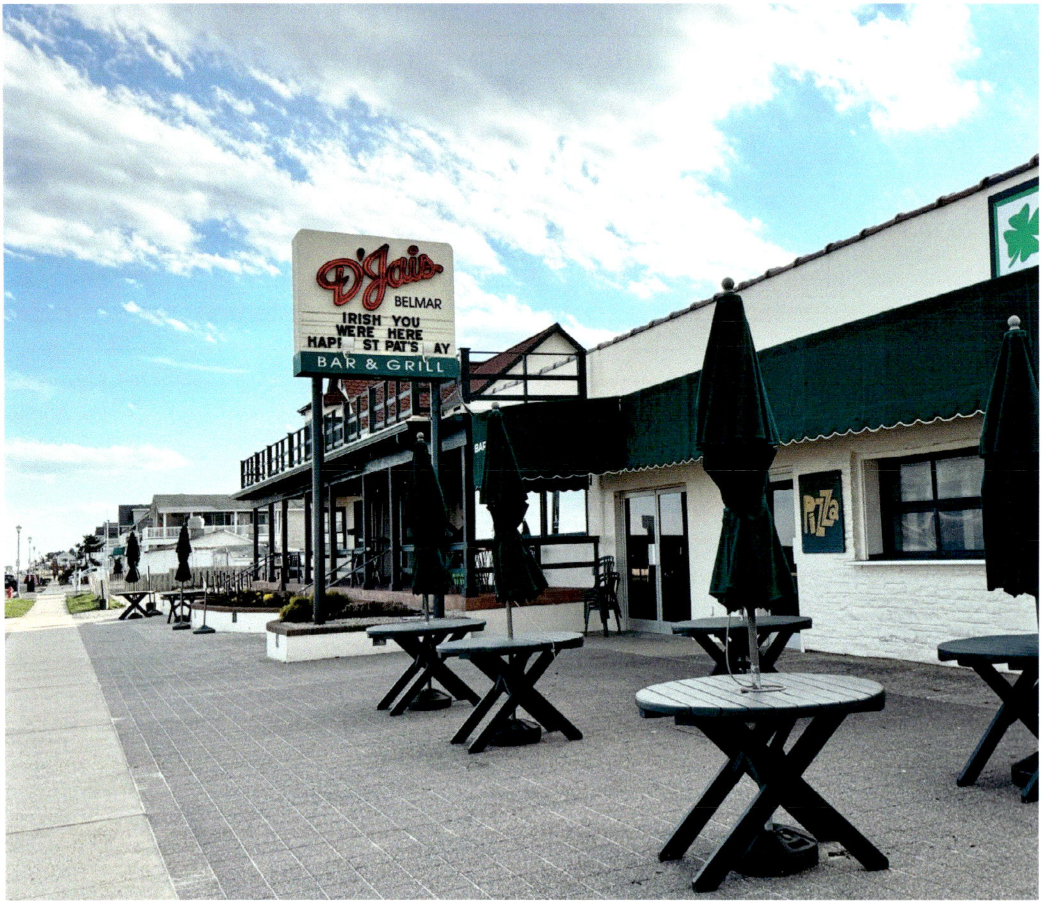

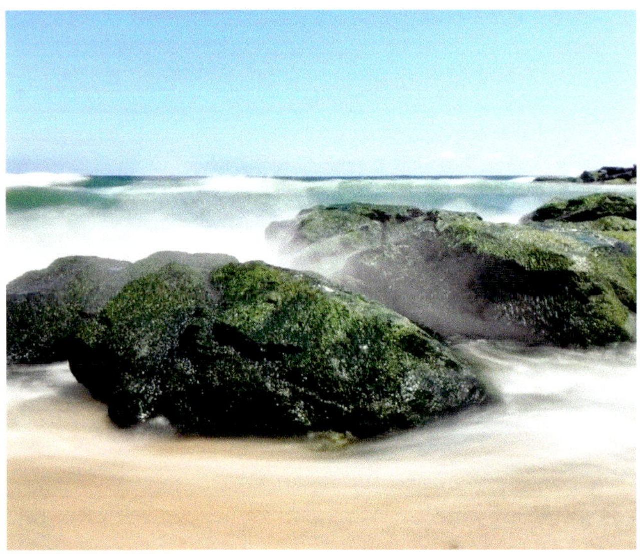

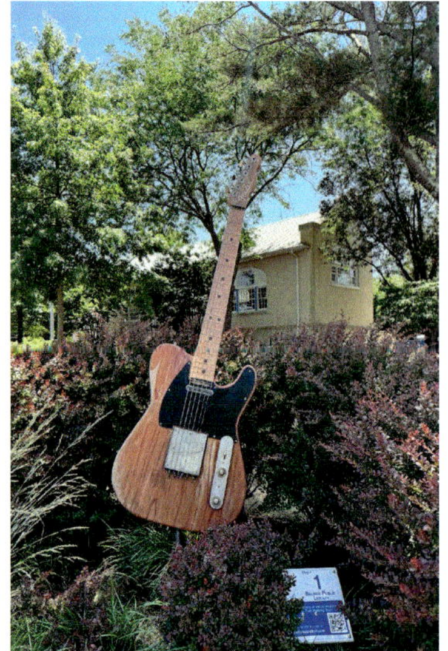

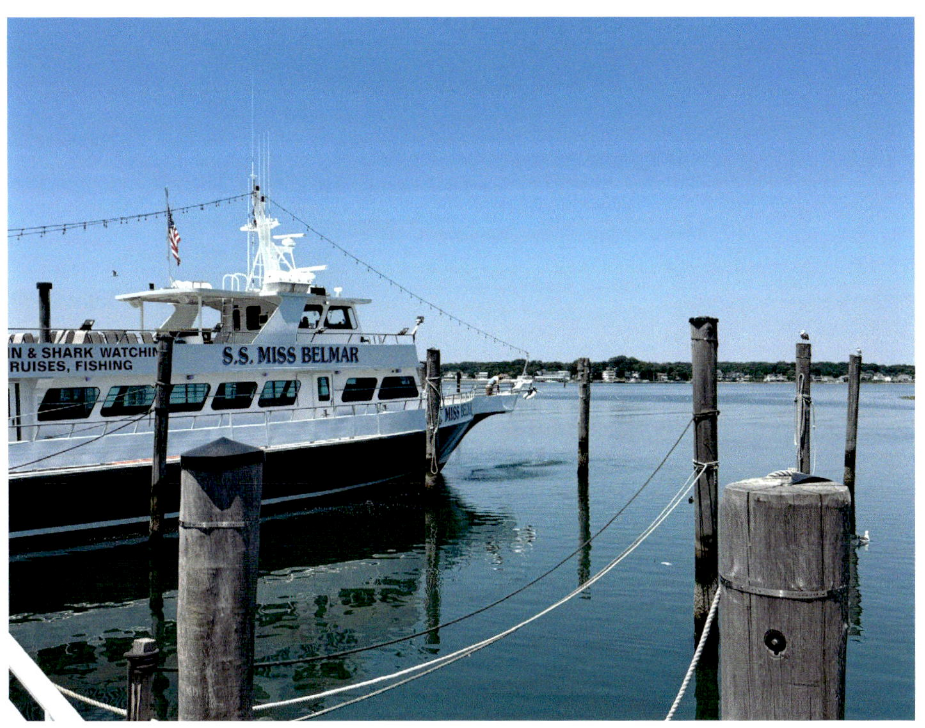
S.S. MISS BELMAR
N & SHARK WATCHIN
RUISES, FISHING

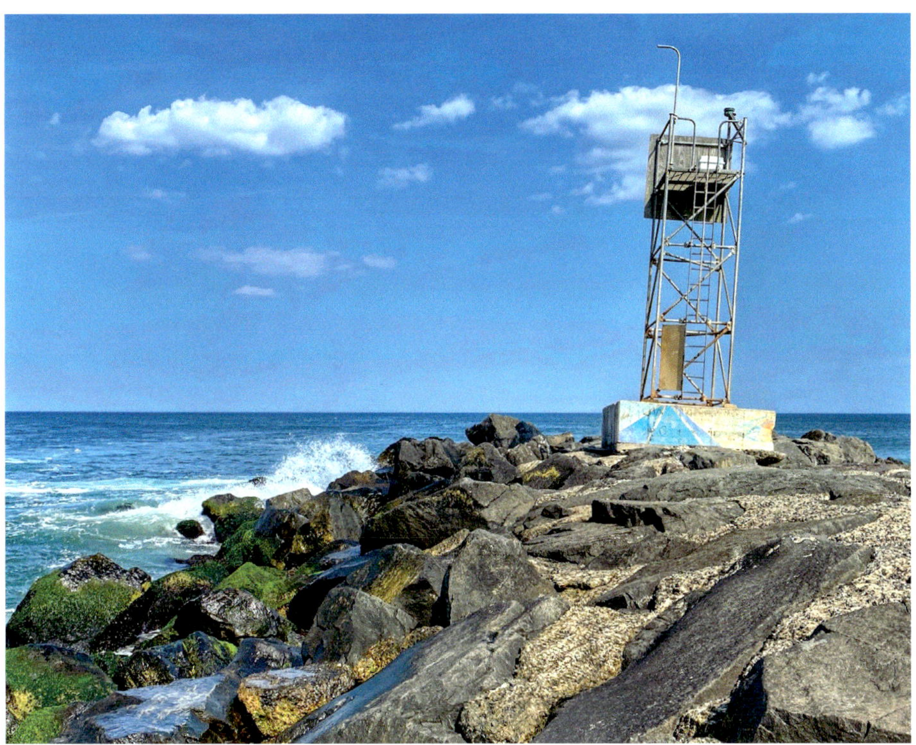

SPRING LAKE

Incorporated:	1892
Motto:	None
Origin of the name:	Named for a clear spring-fed lake, then known as Fresh Creek Pond
Formed from:	Portions of Wall Township
Previous names:	None

Spring Lake was originally laid out into four sections: Villa Park, Spring Lake Beach, Como, and the Brightens, each with a large hotel as the center of the community. The city planners then built lavish estates, or "cottages" to attract the high society of New York and Philadelphia, similarly to the summer "cottages" of Newport, Rhode Island. Over the years, more large estates and even bigger hotels were constructed, and when the rail line was extended south from Long Branch in 1875, the town saw rapid growth. Some of the grand hotels included the Essex Sussex Hotel, the Villa Park House, the Monmouth House, the Breakers, the Carleton Hotel, the Normandy Inn, and the Lake House. Spring Lake is affectionately known as the "Irish Riviera" due to the large amount of Irish American residents—one of the highest percentages in the country. Today, Spring Lake remains a quaint, picturesque community, enjoyed by locals, day-trippers, and summer visitors.

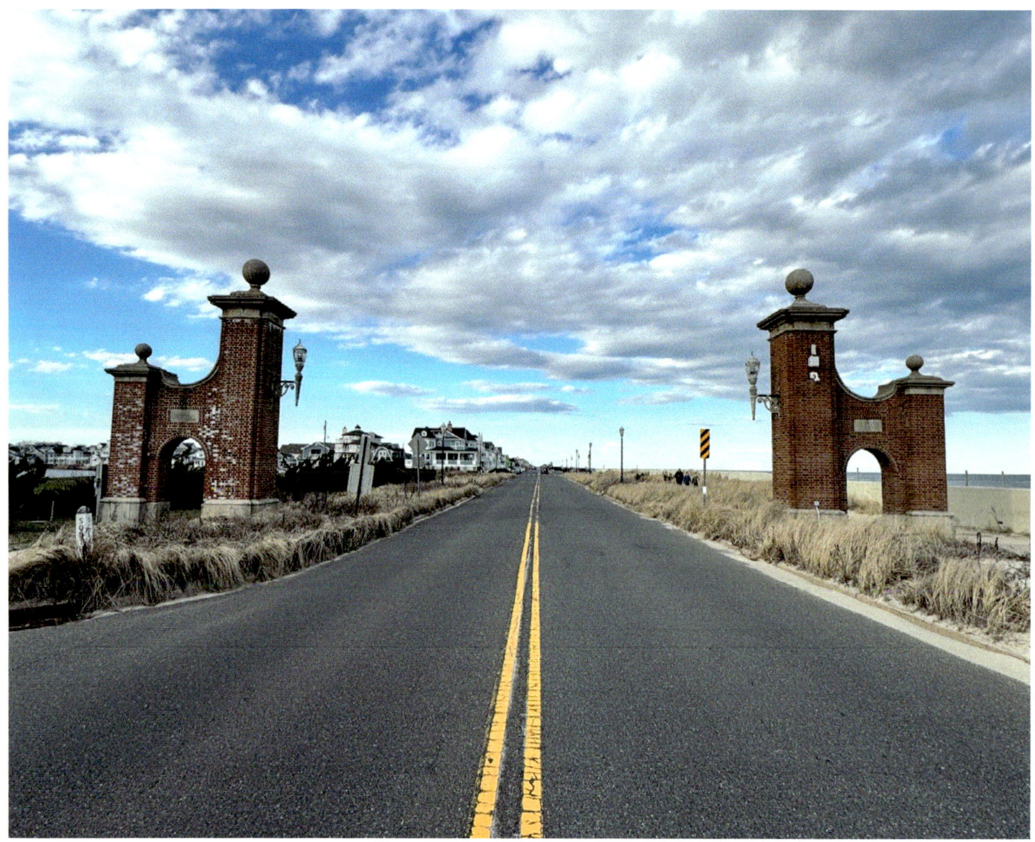

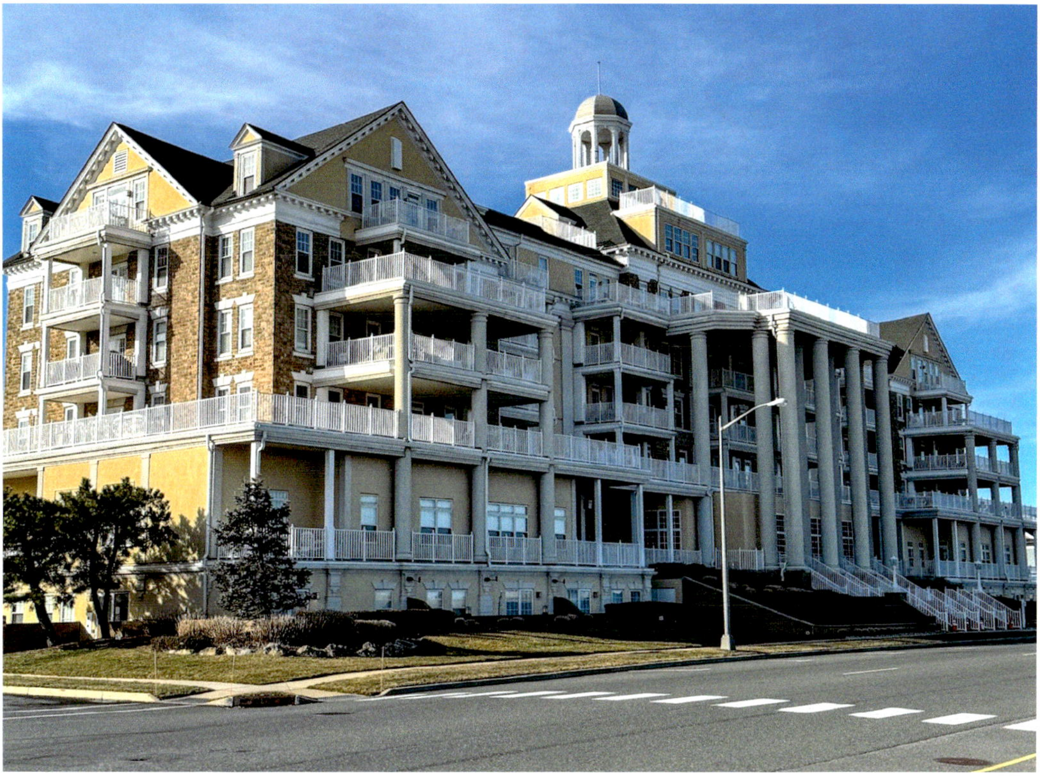

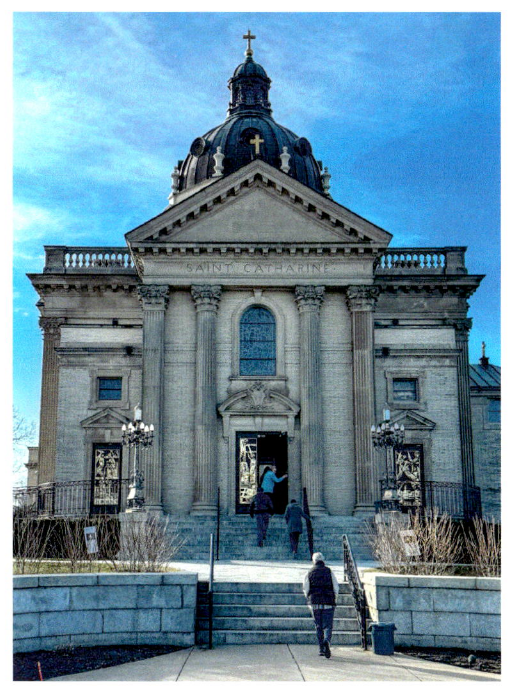

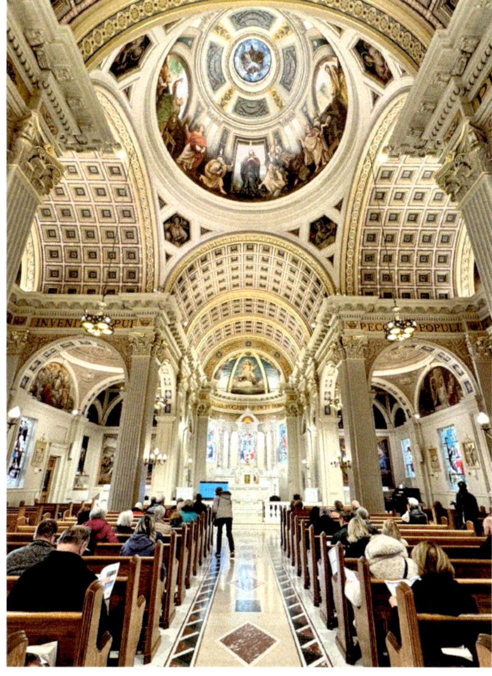

SEA GIRT

Incorporated:	1917
Motto:	"Where the Cedars Meet the Sea"
Origin of the name:	Commodore Stockton named his estate *Sea Girt*, because it was surrounded by water on three sides
Formed from:	Portions of Wall Township
Previous names:	None

In 1853, Commodore Robert F. Stockton purchased farmland in present-day Sea Girt from Dr. Charles Montrose Graham and Mr. John Sherman and built a large estate for his family. Years later, a group of developers from Philadelphia bought more land and the population began to grow. In 1887, the federal government bought 120 acres along the coast and established a training ground for the New Jersey National Guard, called "Camp Sea Girt," which is still in use today. Guardsmen here were trained in preparation for the Spanish-American War, World War I, and World War II. The original 1850s farmhouse on the grounds was used as a summer residence for the governor, until 1904, when a new house "arrived" on the site. After the 1904 World's Fair in St. Louis, the New Jersey Headquarters building was disassembled and transported to Camp Sea Girt, reassembled and served as the governor's summer residence from 1906–1941. It was demolished in 1971. 1897, Sea Girt Lighthouse was erected. Its beacon tower is built into the keeper's house, the last of its kind on the Atlantic Coast. Sea Girt is home to the Parker House and Rod's Tavern, two well-known Jersey Shore establishments.

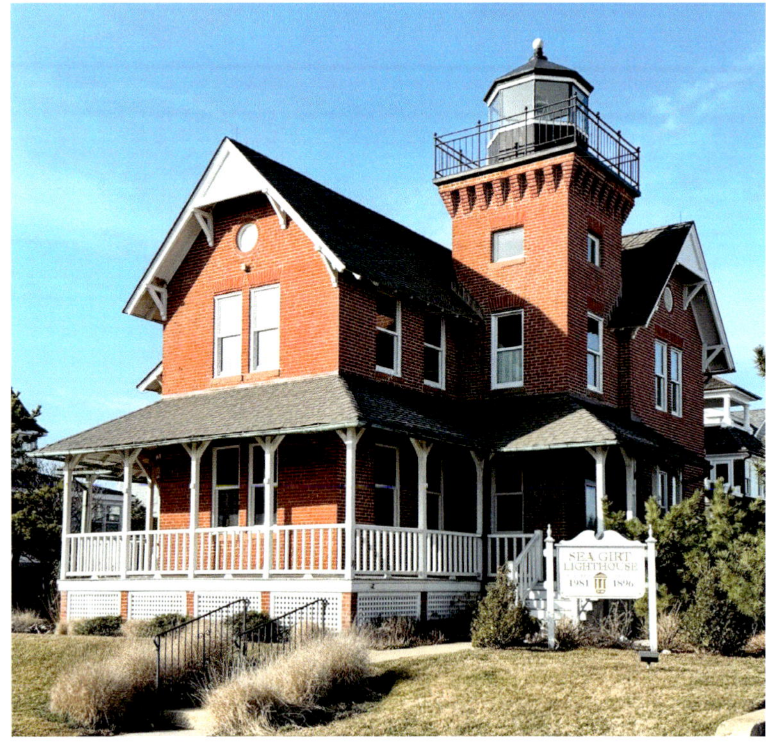

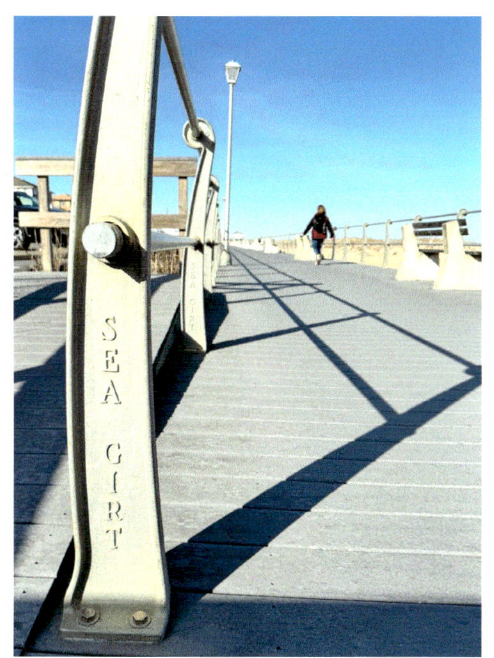

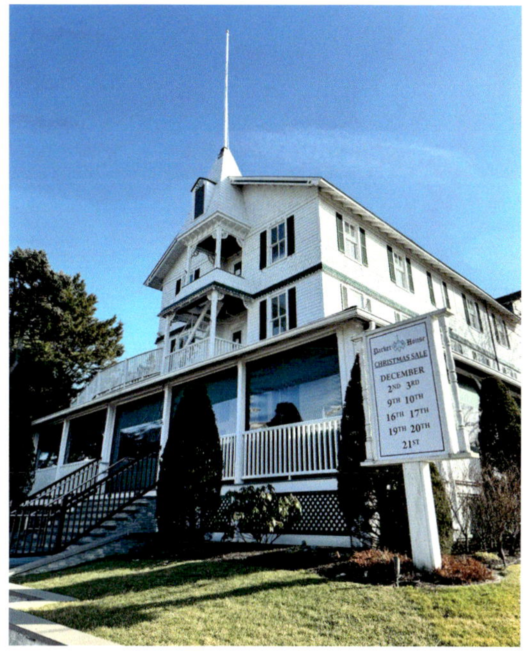

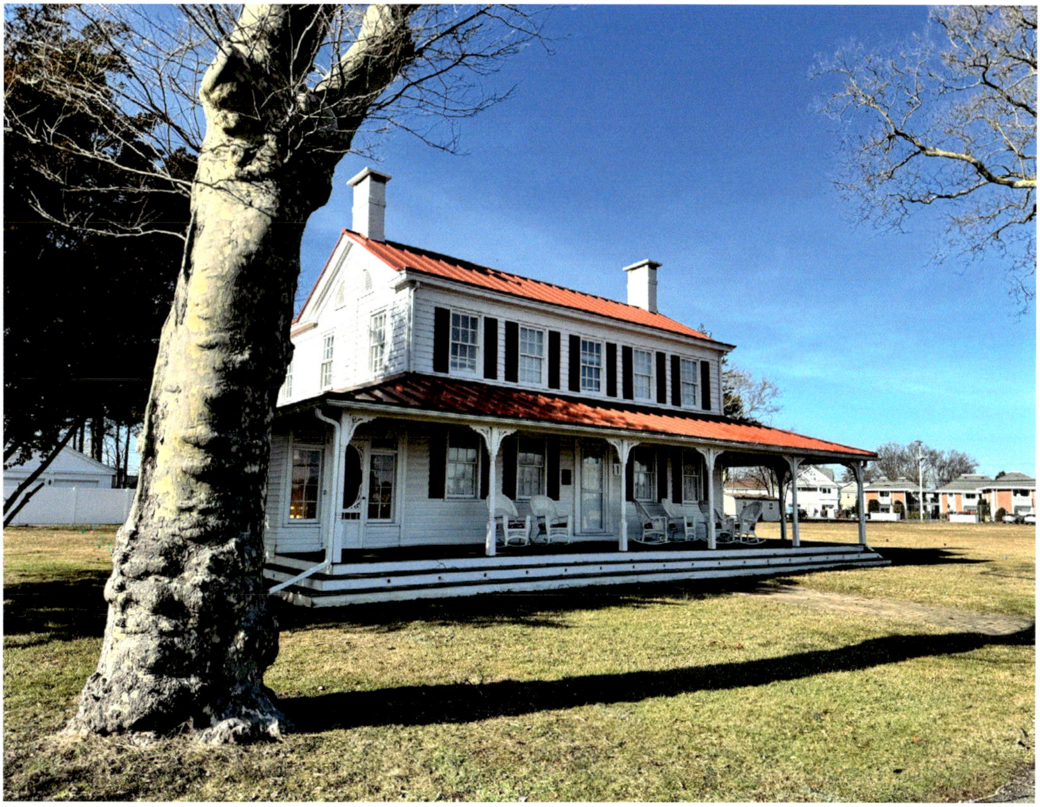

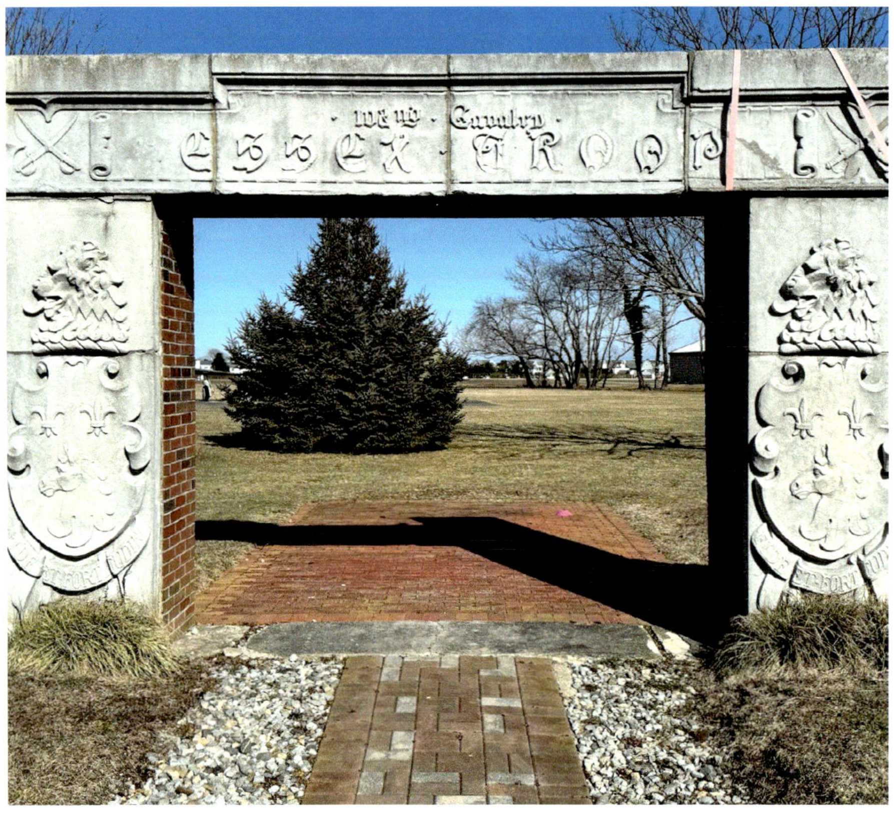

MANASQUAN

Incorporated: 1887
Motto: None
Origin of the name: From the Lenape "Mënàskunk," meaning "place to gather grass or
                         reeds" or "stream of the island of Squaws"
Formed from: Portions of Wall Township
Previous names: Squan Village, Crabtown

One of the earliest known businesses in the Manasquan area was a tavern owned by Jacob Curtis around 1815. A stagecoach route was established in 1850 from New York to Manasquan, followed by rail lines, which connected the quiet beach village to Philadelphia, New York, and Northern New Jersey. This allowed the population to expand through the second half of the nineteenth century. Fishing has always been a staple for the people of Manasquan, with an abundance of bluefish, fluke, and stripers. A busy commercial district grew along Main Street, full of eateries, ice cream parlors, and coffee shops. Several bars and restaurants in Manasquan make it a great place for nightlife, including the Osprey Night Club, Leggetts Sand Bar, Lubranos, and the Squan Tavern. Heading south, the town (and Monmouth County) comes to an abrupt, but scenic end at the Manasquan Inlet.

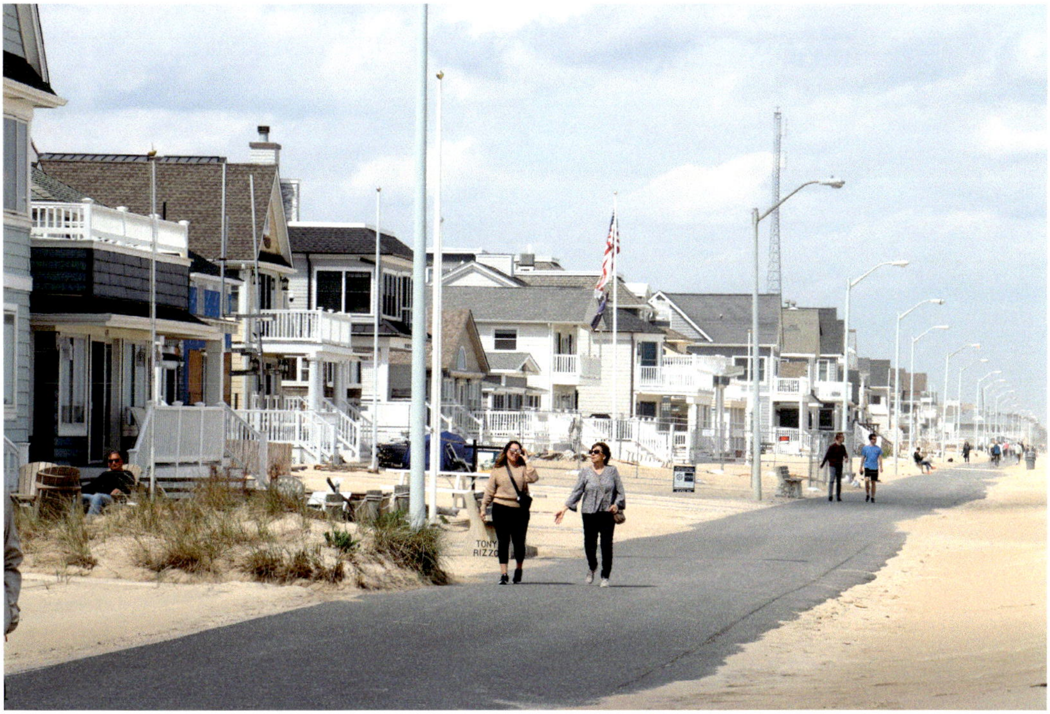

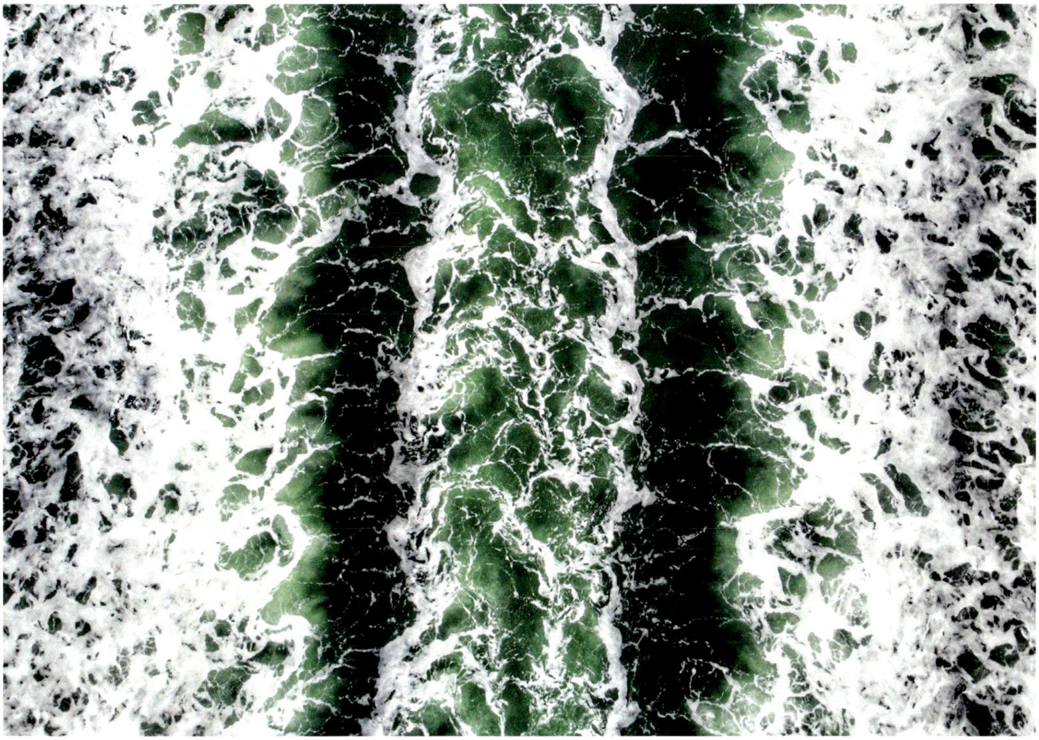

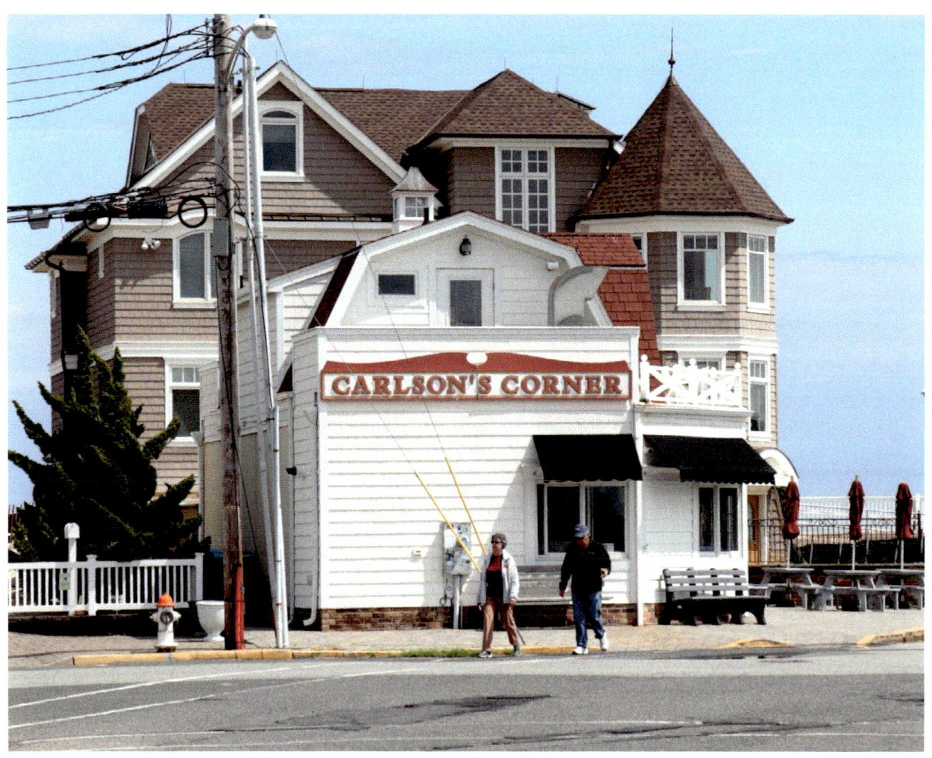

CARLSON'S CORNER

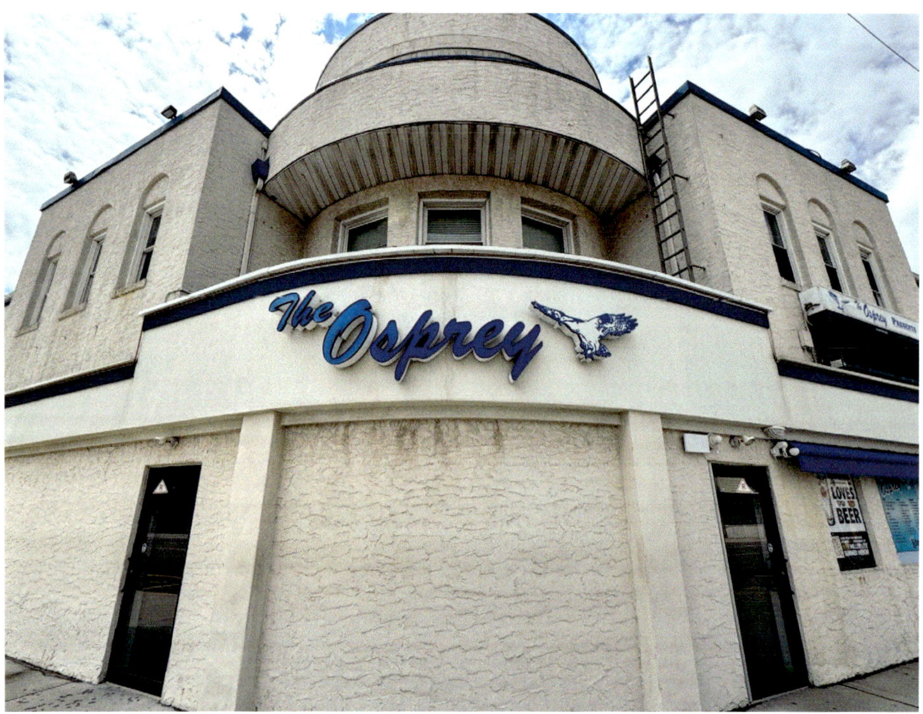

The Osprey

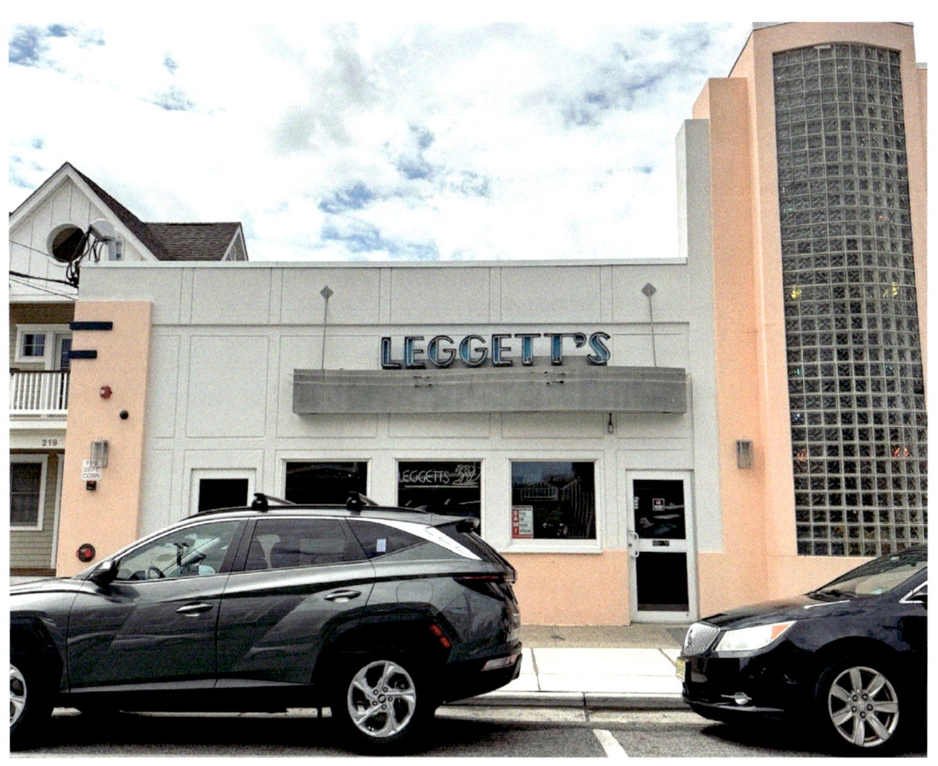
LEGGETT'S

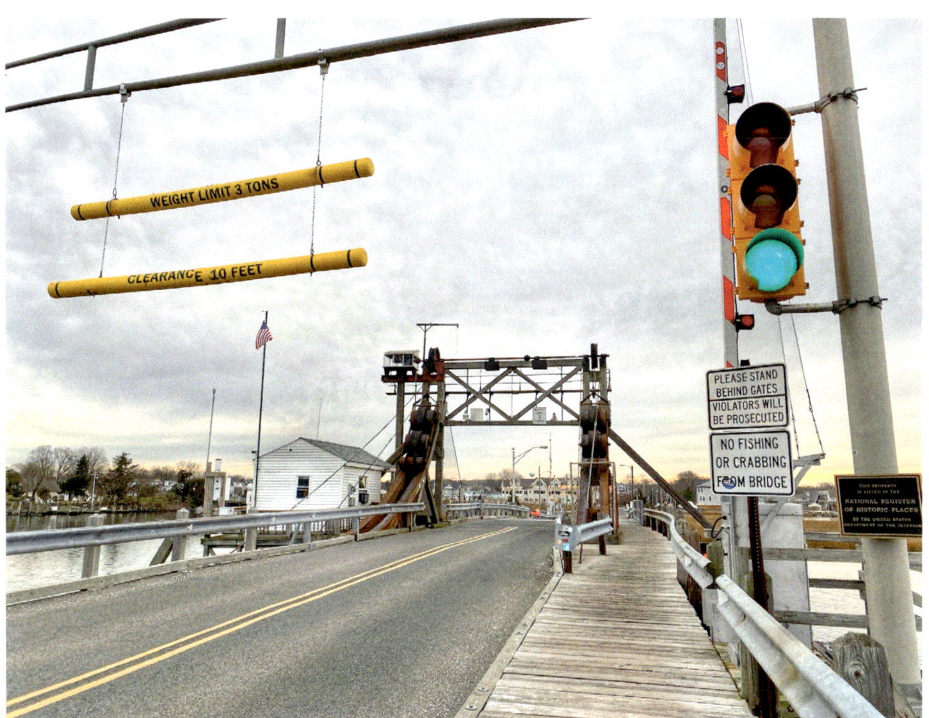
WEIGHT LIMIT 3 TONS
CLEARANCE 10 FEET
PLEASE STAND
BEHIND GATES
VIOLATORS WILL
BE PROSECUTED
NO FISHING
OR CRABBING
FROM BRIDGE

2

OCEAN COUNTY

Heading south down the coast, the county begins in the middle of the Manasquan Inlet. All of the county's shorefront communities occupy one of two barrier islands: Barnegat Peninsula to the north (from Point Pleasant Beach to Island Beach State Park) and Long Beach Island to the south. Route 35 is the main artery of travel from Point Pleasant Beach to Seaside Park. Ocean County's largest body of water is Barnegat Bay, which runs for 42 miles between the mainland and barrier islands. In fact, more than 30 percent of the county is water.

POINT PLEASANT BEACH

Incorporated:	1886
Motto:	"Top of the Inland Waterway"
Origin of the name:	Named after its location at the top point of Barnegat Peninsula
Formed from:	Portions of Brick Township
Previous names:	Squan Beach

Point Pleasant Beach is a distinct community from Point Pleasant Borough, although both seceded from Brick Township more than 100 years ago. Most of Point Pleasant Beach is contained east of Route 35, while some of the community lies west on the shores of the Manasquan River. The first settlers in the area were European Quakers in the early 1700s; most were fishermen and farmers. Point Pleasant Beach is the northern terminus of what was once called "Squan Beach," the former name of the Barnegat Peninsula. Between 1870 and 1880, Captain John Arnold built a road to the ocean (present-day Arnold Avenue) and helped convince the Central Jersey Railroad to extend its service to Point Pleasant Beach. The first permanent boardwalk was installed in 1915, but the southern portion of it was washed away by a hurricane in 1938. Charles Jenkinson was instrumental in turning the quiet Point Pleasant boardwalk into a bustling center of entertainment, when he opened an oceanfront pavilion in 1928. Jenkinson's Pavilion and the surrounding boardwalk area would eventually feature a candy shop, soda fountain, dance hall, swimming pool, and miniature golf. His son Orlo continued to add to the attractions by building a miniature train ride on the beach in 1949, connecting the pavilion with the inlet, which lasted nearly fifty years. In the late '70s, Pat Storino bought Jenkinson's and continued to expand attractions, eventually adding more rides, restaurants, an aquarium, arcades, bars, water slides, and even rebuilding the pavilion when the original burned down in 1989. Point Pleasant Beach continues to attract thousands of visitors each summer, whether it be to fish along the "wall" and jetties of the inlet, or to enjoy the bars and fresh seafood restaurants, such as Martell's Tiki Bar, the Shrimp Box, Spike's Fish Market, the Lobster Shanty, and Jenkinson's Pavilion Bar and Restaurant.

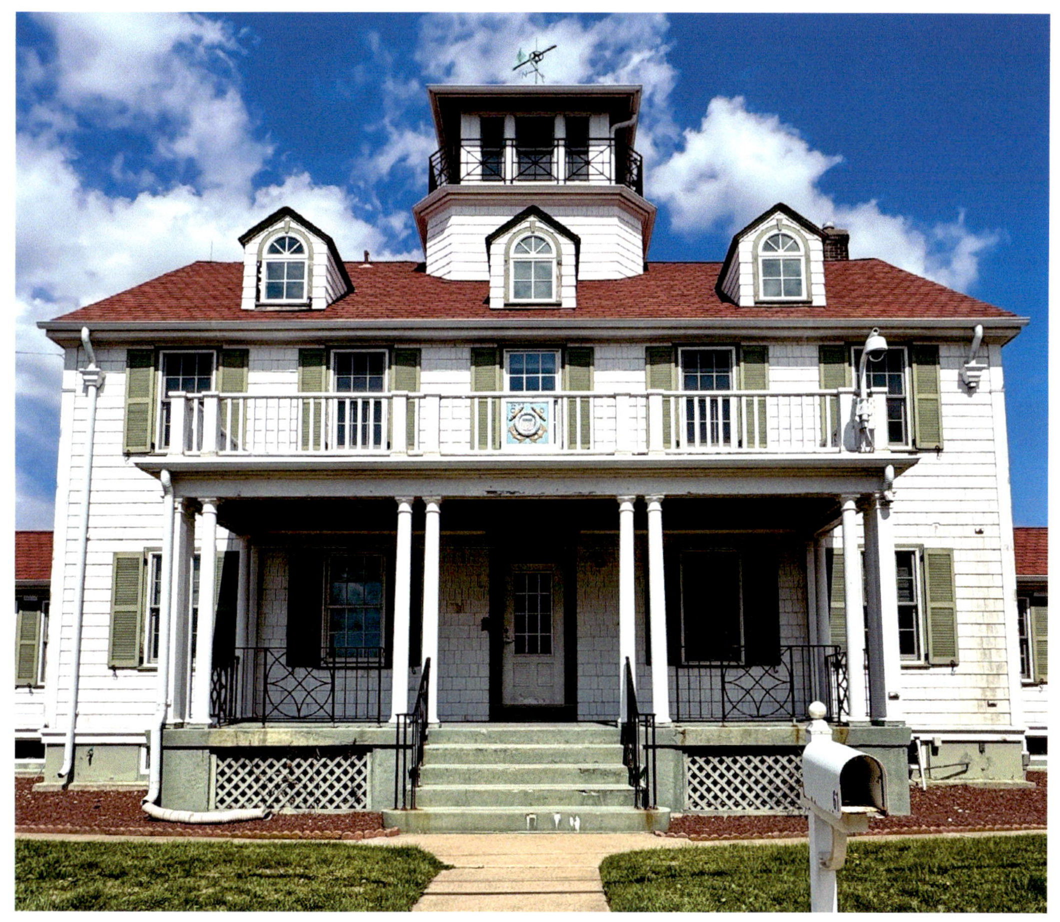

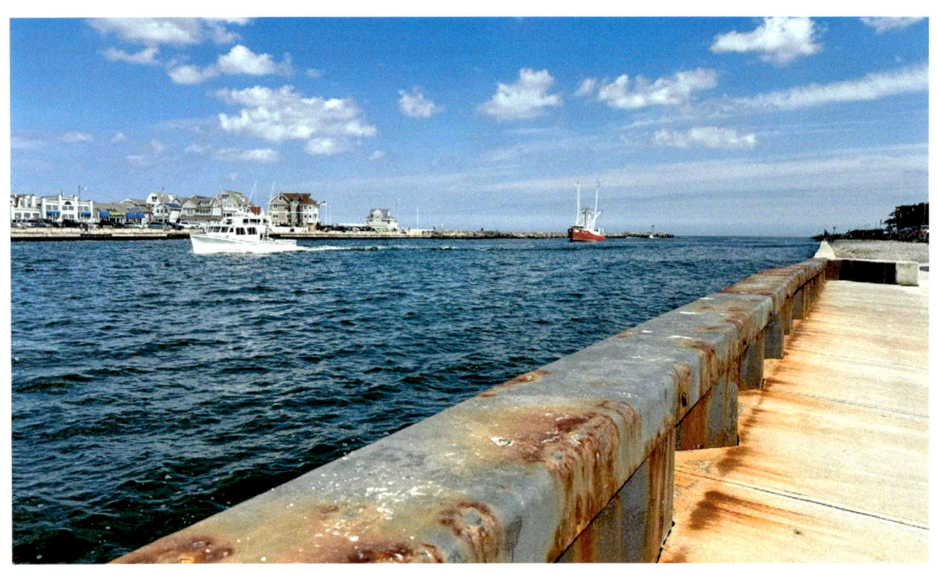

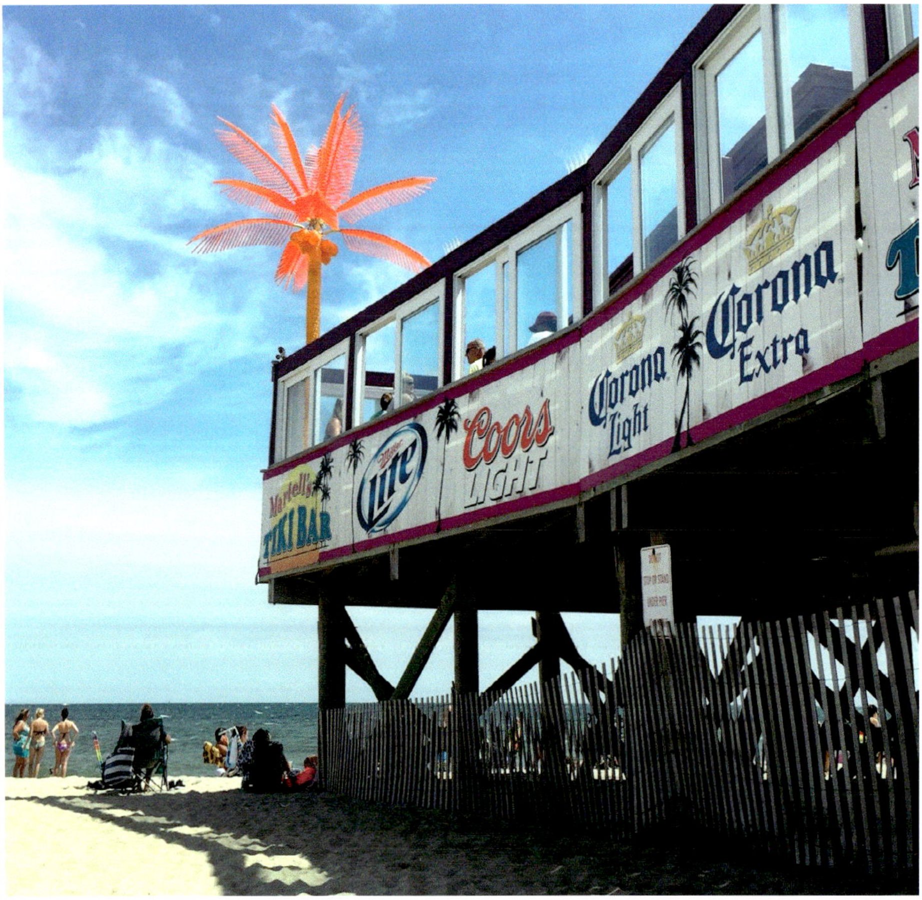

Martell's
TIKI BAR
lite
Coors
LIGHT
Corona
Light
Corona
Extra

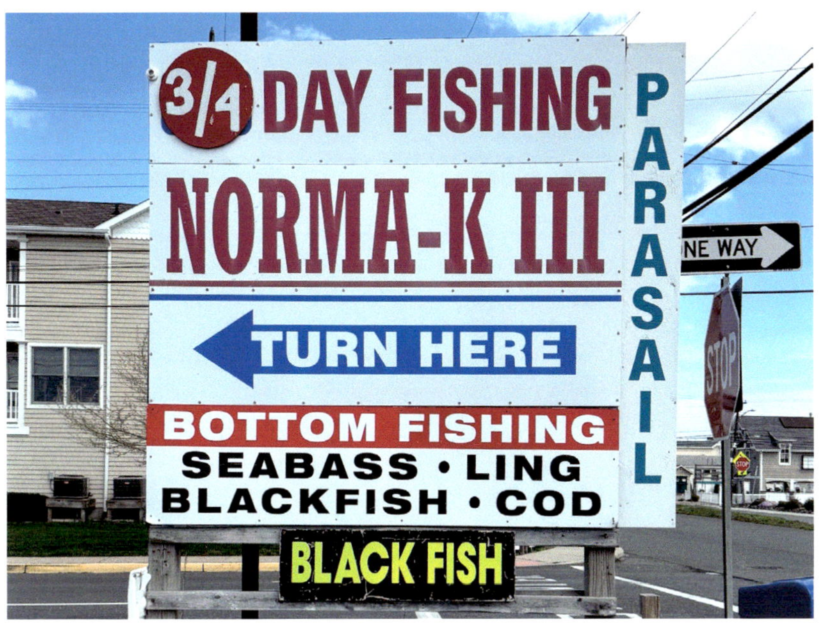
3/4 DAY FISHING
NORMA-K III
TURN HERE
BOTTOM FISHING
SEABASS • LING
BLACKFISH • COD
BLACK FISH
PARASAIL
NE WAY
STOP

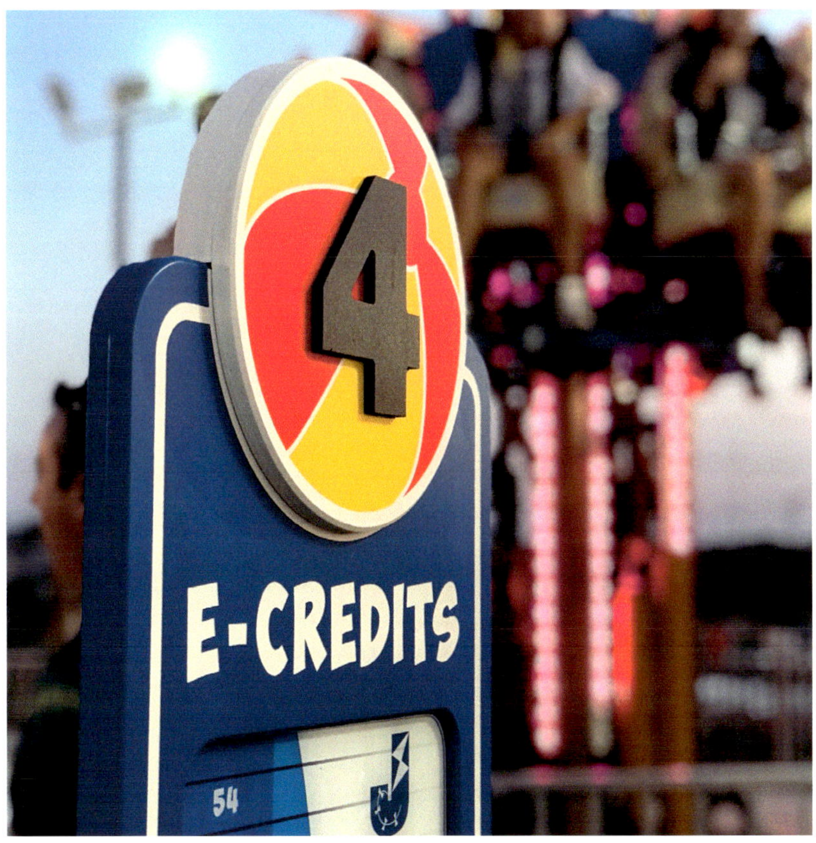
4
E-CREDITS
54

BAY HEAD

Incorporated: 1886
Motto: None
Origin of the name: Named after the Bayhead Land Company which established the community; also, its location at the "head" of Barnegat Bay
Formed from: Portions of Brick Township
Previous names: Squan Beach

Edward Howe, William Harris, and David Mount, founding partners in the Bayhead Land Company, bought land in present-day Bay Head in 1879 with the goal of creating a resort town for wealthy families from New York and Philadelphia. A 4,000-foot-long seawall was built to protect their assets from mother nature (this wall would be covered by sand and forgotten for decades; however, it played a huge role in protecting Bay Head from Hurricane Sandy in 2012). The founders were also successful in getting train service to Bay Head from New York and Pennsylvania in the 1880s. Anyone visiting Bay Head today must stop at Mueller's Bakery, who has been serving their world-famous crumb cake since 1890.

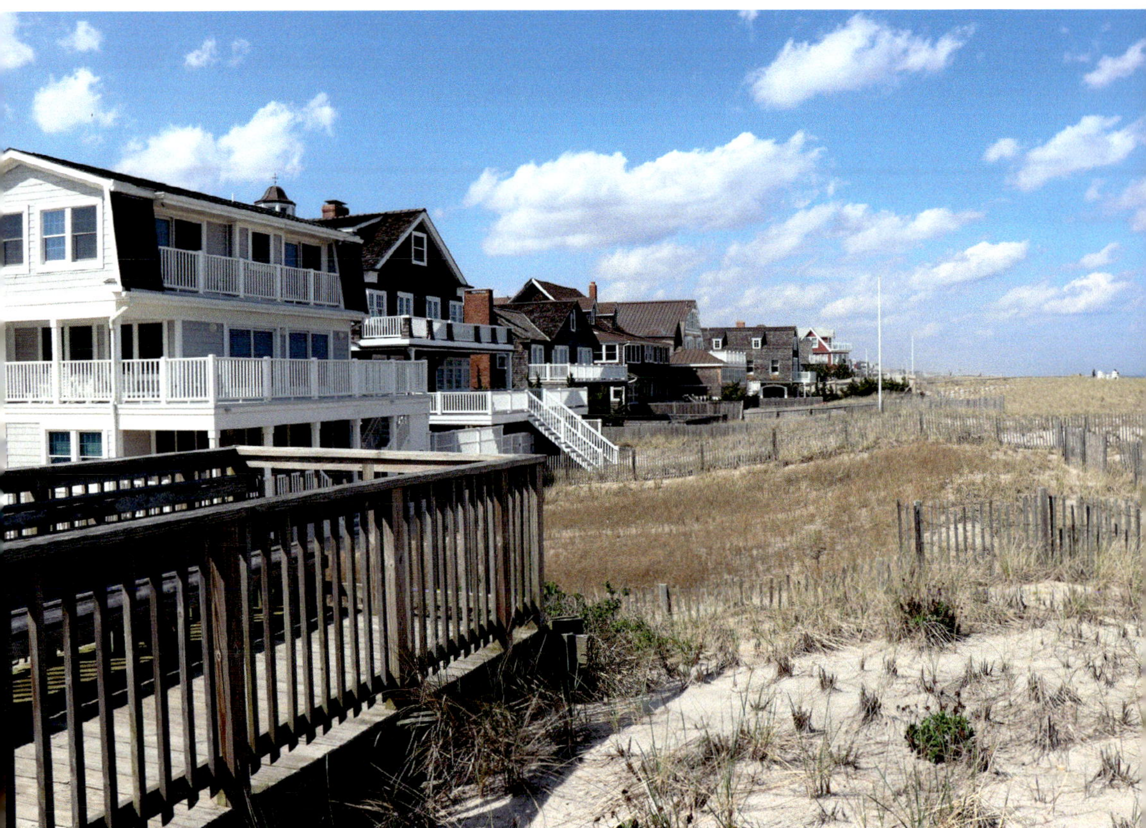

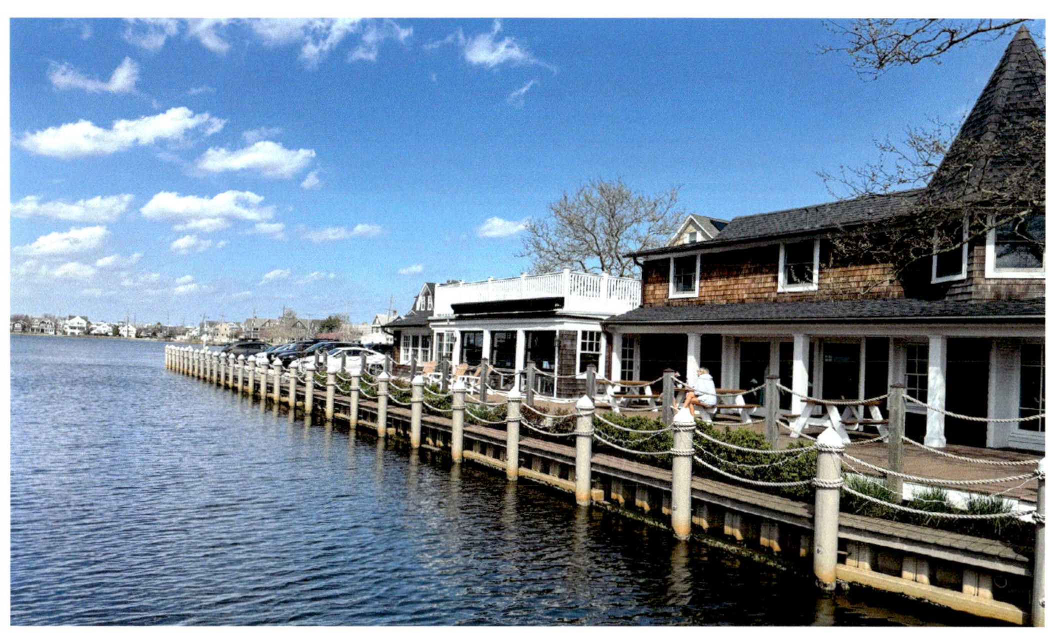

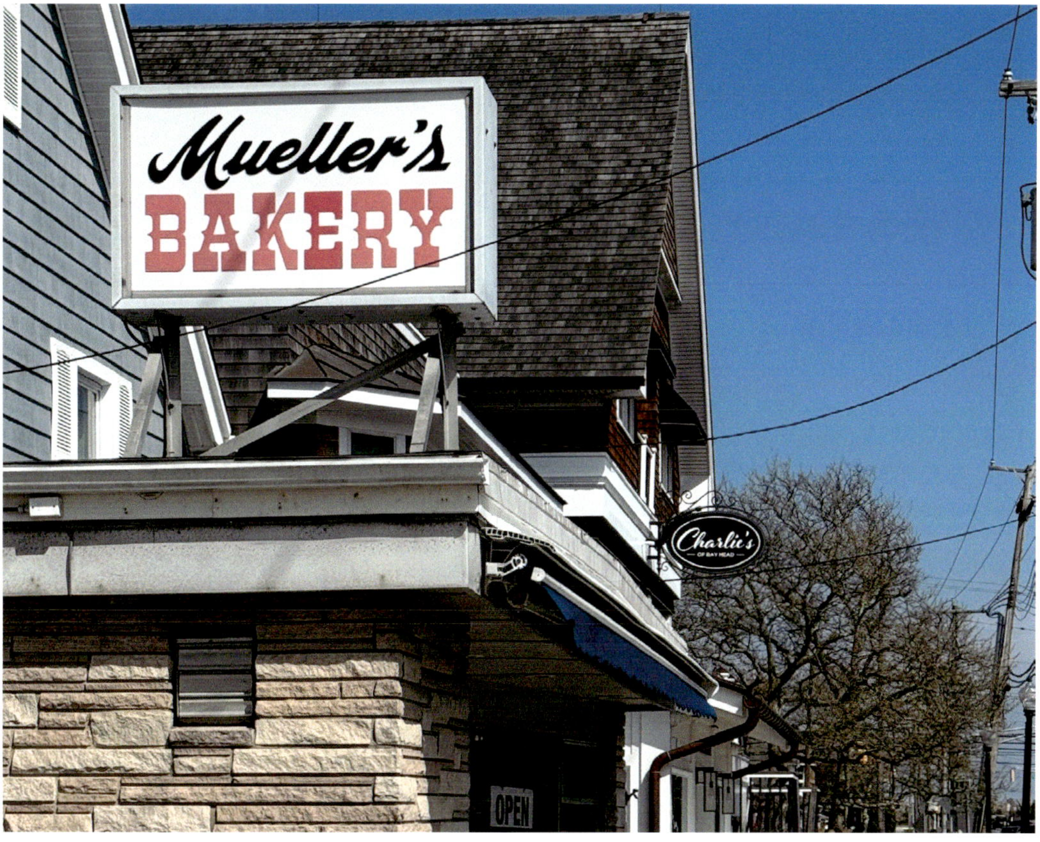

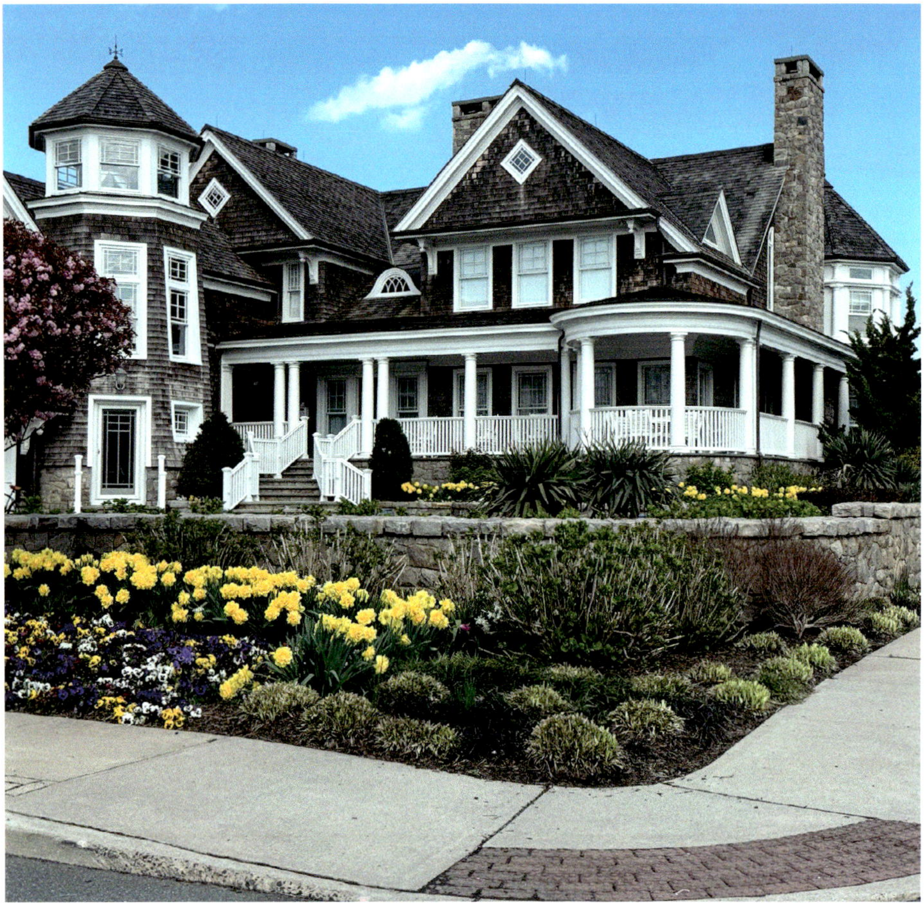

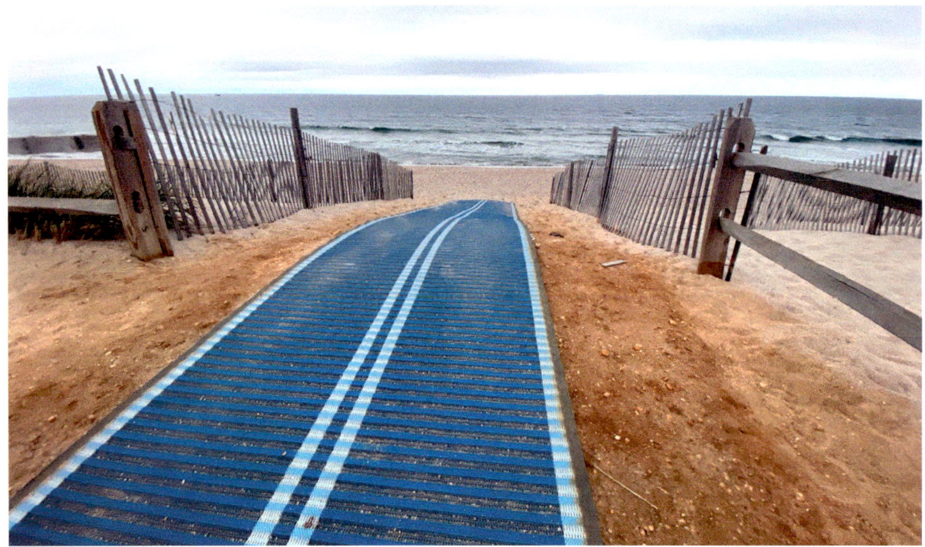

MANTOLOKING

Incorporated: 1911
Motto: None
Origin of the name: From the Lenape words for "sand place" and/or "frog ground"
Formed from: Portions of Brick Township
Previous names: Squan Beach

Large acres of property were purchased by Frederick Downer and Frank Hall in 1875. They donated some of the land to the Mantoloking Golf/Yacht Club, the Water Company, and the Church of St. Simon-by-The-Sea. Eventually, all the land in the area was titled to the Seashore Land Company and Seashore Improvement Company. In 1882, Captain John Arnold, of Point Pleasant fame, was tasked with the development of Mantoloking, and his first order of business was to build the first bridge to the mainland in 1884. The northern end of Mantoloking was the last to be developed, because there was no road connecting it to Bay Head and other towns to the north. One was built in 1908, and the rest of the community was eventually developed. Over the years, the town held true to its original blueprint, no shopping districts, boardwalks, parking lots, businesses, or amusements. No alcohol is permitted to be sold. Mantoloking is, and has always been known for its large, stately homes with decorative landscaping along the ocean and bay, many of which were obliterated during Hurricane Sandy in 2012. In fact, the storm's surge was so strong, it created a new inlet by the bridge where the ocean met the bay (which was eventually filled in).

Together, Mantoloking and Bay Head are known as "the gold coast" of the Jersey Shore.

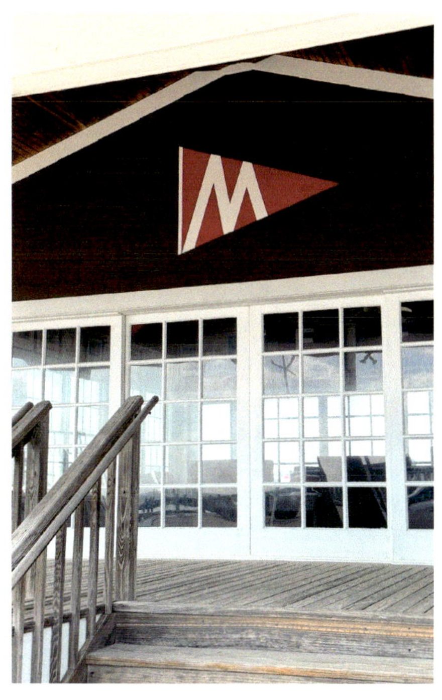
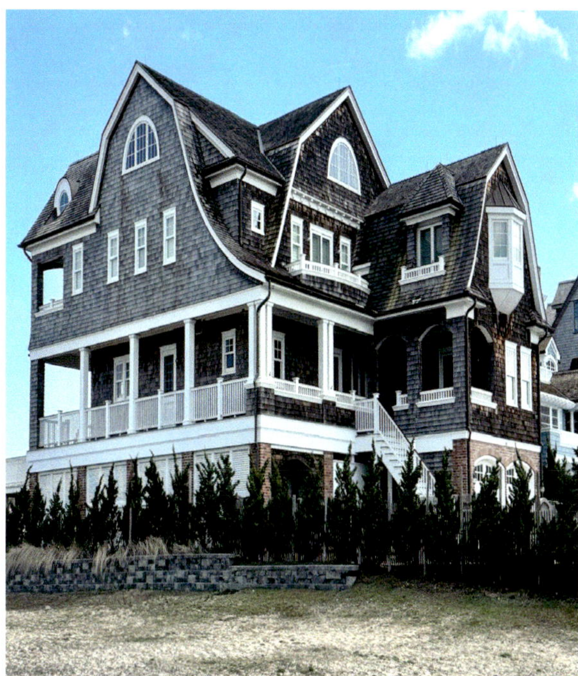

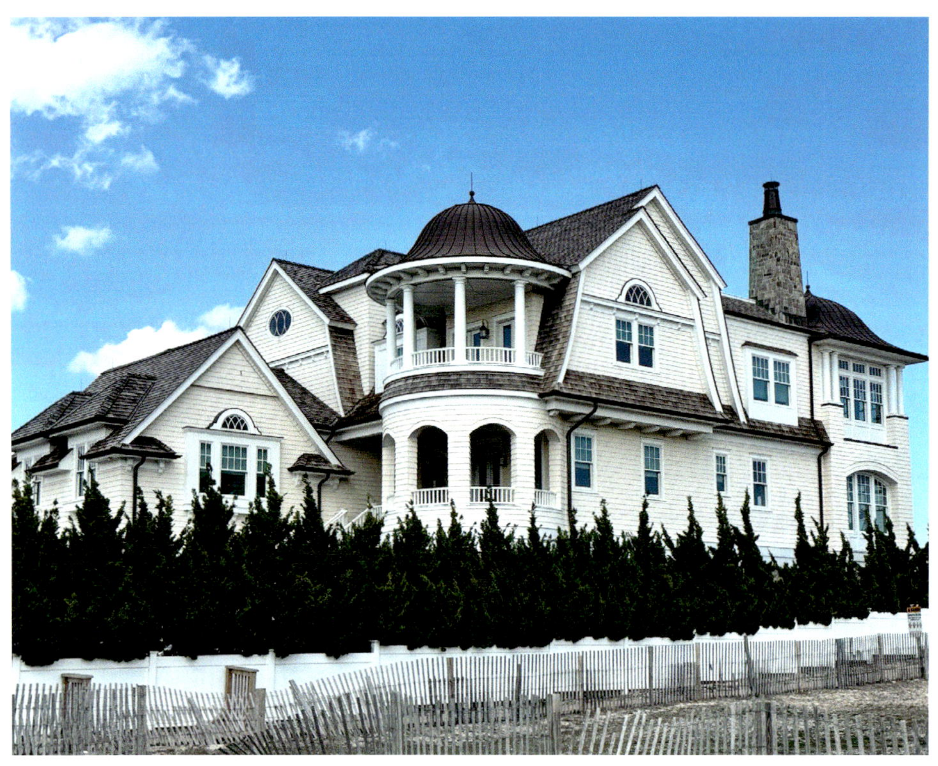

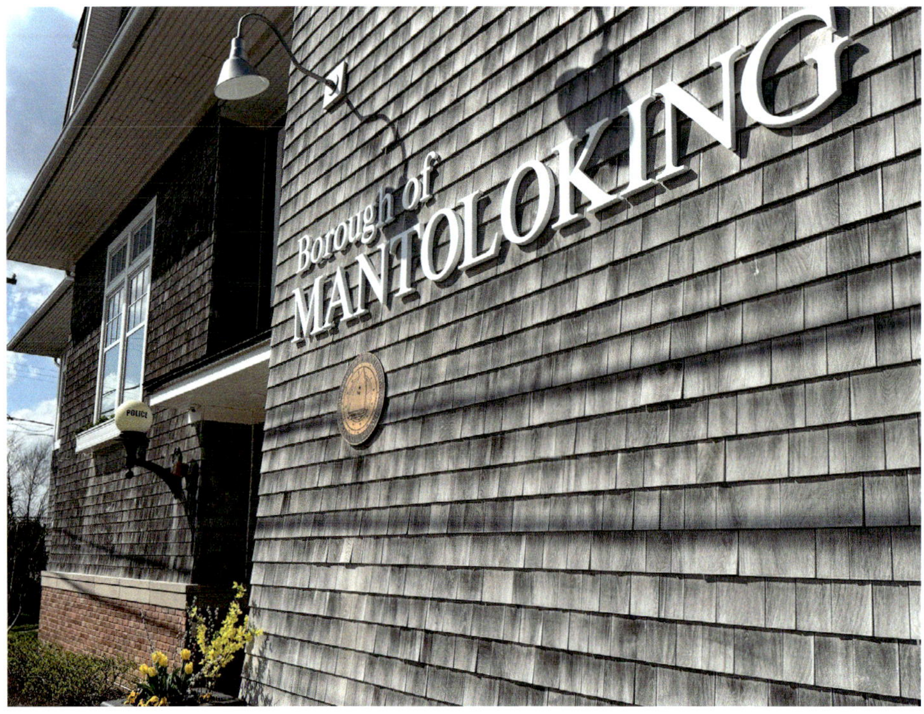
Borough of
MANTOLOKING
POLICE

BRICK TOWNSHIP: BRICK BEACH I, II, III, NORMANDY BEACH (NORTH)

Incorporated:	1850
Motto:	Bricktown USA
Origin of the name:	Named in honor of Joseph W. Brick, local citizen and owner of Bergen Iron Works
Formed from:	Portions of Dover Township and Howell Township
Previous names:	Squan Beach, the villages of Adamston, Burrsville, Laurelton, Cedarbridge, Herbertsville, Osbornville

While most of Brick sits on the mainland, a tiny portion of the township reaches the Atlantic Ocean—these communities are referred to as Brick Beach I, II, III, and the northern portion of Normandy Beach. In the early twentieth century, Brick had much more beachfront property, but when Mantoloking left the township in 1911, it left these small beaches seemingly isolated from the rest of the community. Just south of Brick Beach III is Normandy Beach, whose northern half is governed by Brick, and southern portion managed by Toms River.

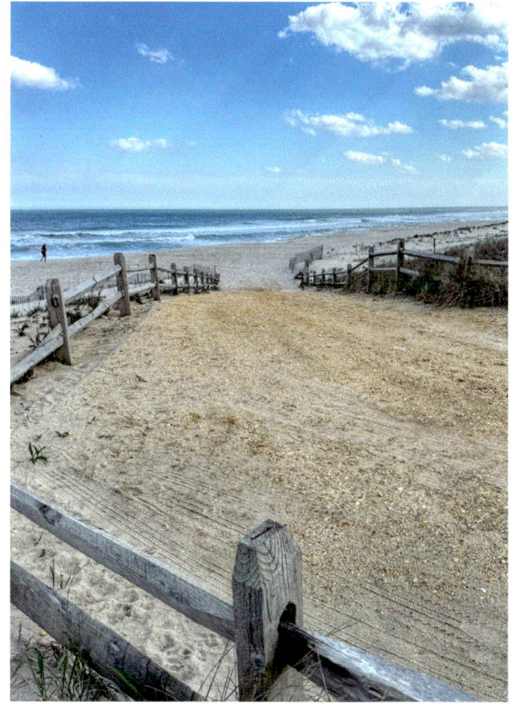

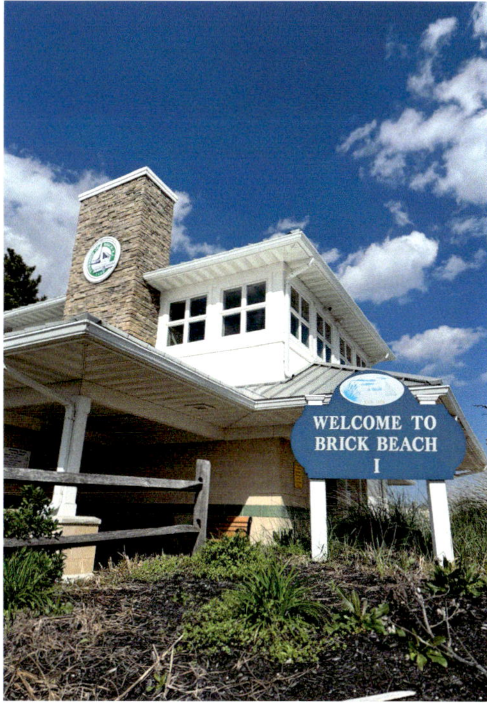

DOVER BEACHES NORTH (TOMS RIVER): NORMANDY BEACH (SOUTH), SILVER BEACH, CHADWICK BEACH, SEACREST BEACH, MONTEREY BEACH, OCEAN BEACHES 1, 2, AND 3

Incorporated: 1798
Motto: None
Origin of the name: Named in honor of Dover, England
Formed from: Portions of Shrewsbury Township
Previous names: Squan Beach, Goose Creek, Goose Neck Creek, Tom's Creek, Dover Township

Toms River was originally incorporated as Dover Township in 1798. Through a referendum in 2006, residents voted for the name to officially be changed to Toms River. The town is split into three separate areas: mainland Toms River, Dover Beaches North, and Dover Beaches South, which are separated by the borough of Lavallette. The area was settled in the early 1800s by the Chadwick family as a fishing village. The completion of the Pennsylvania Railroad on the island, and Route 35 in 1913 led to more and more people settling in the area, now a vacation resort. Most of Dover Beaches North are private beaches, with no public access. Some of the dates these small communities were established are as follows: Normandy Beach 1916, Monterey Beach 1948, and Seacrest Beach 1954.

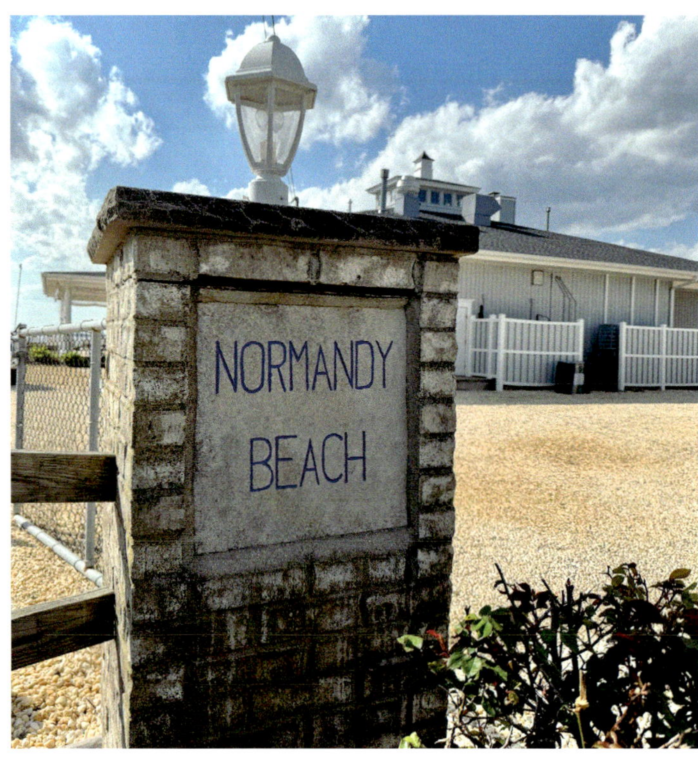

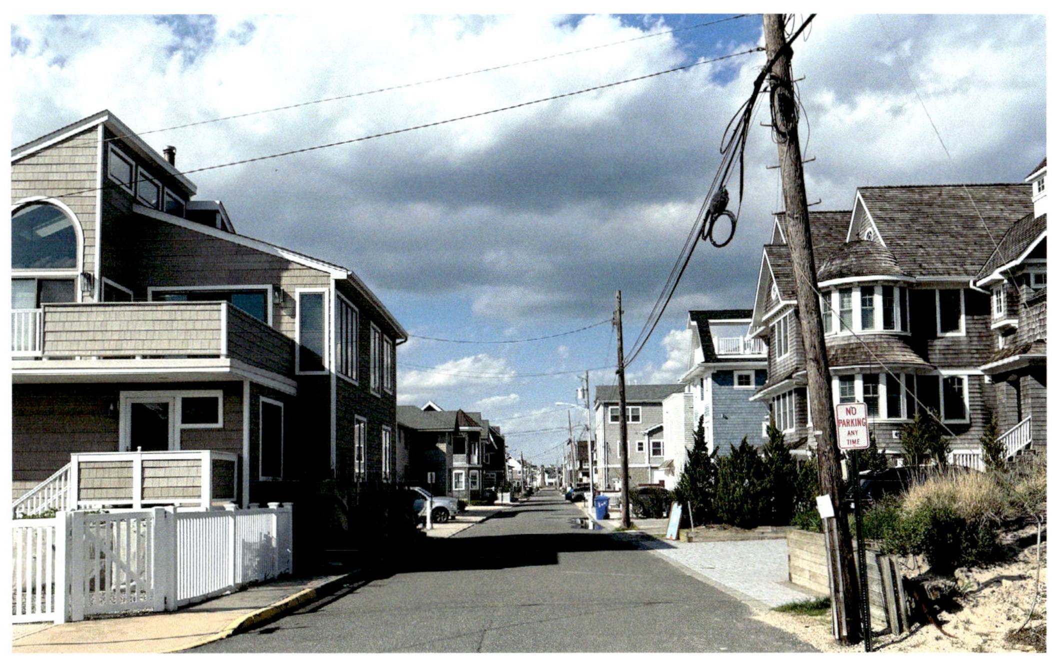

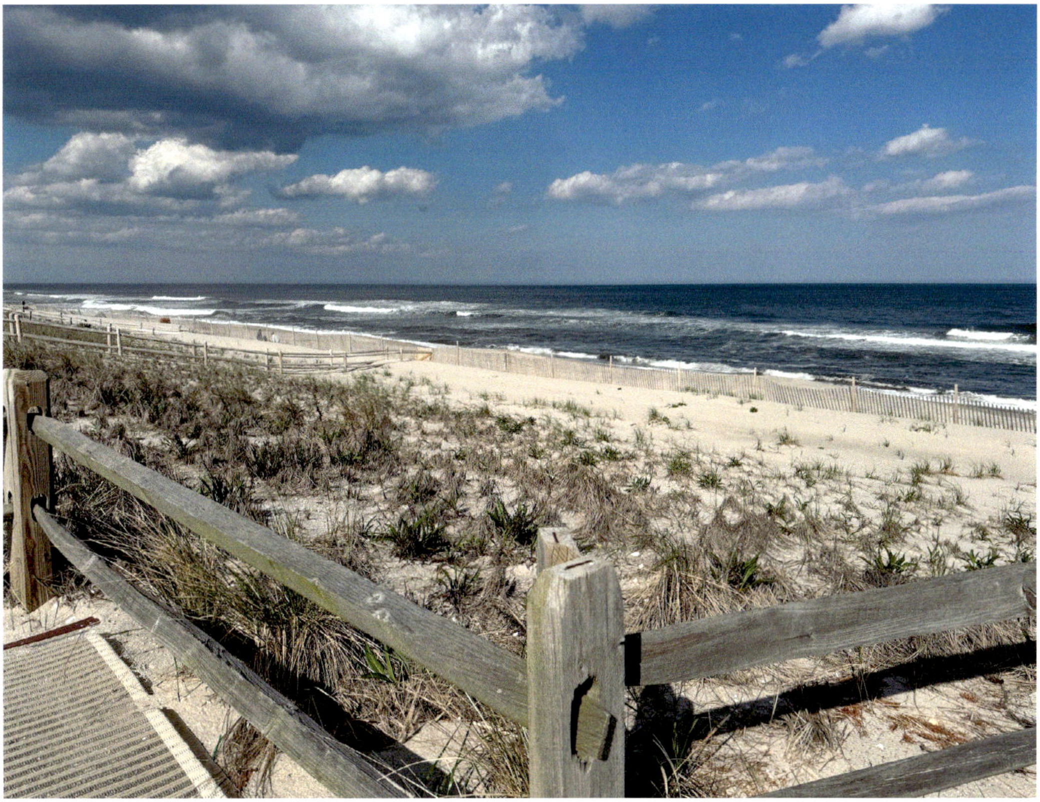

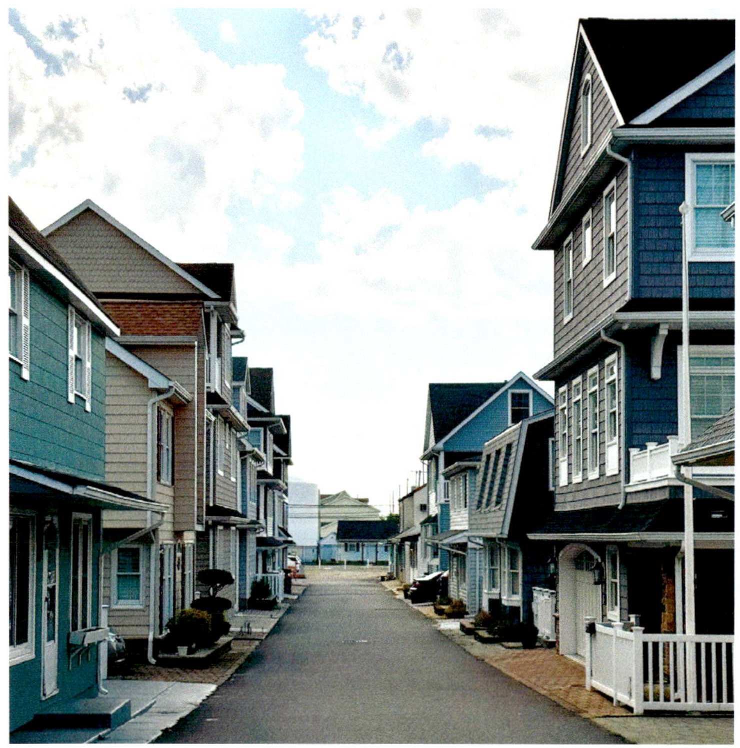

LAVALLETTE

Incorporated:	1887
Motto:	"The Ideal Family Seaside Resort"
Origin of the name:	Named in honor of Admiral Elie A. F. La Vallette and his son, Albert T. Lavallette, founder of the borough
Formed from:	Portions of Dover Township
Previous names:	Squan Beach, Lavallette City by the Sea

Lavallette's beginnings were like many on the barrier island—summer hunting, fishing, and shelling grounds, first by the Lenape, then by European settlers. Temporary camps were built by New Englanders and New Yorkers for fishing and whaling. The borough was only accessible by boat until the railroad was established in 1881, which ran from mainland Toms River across Barnegat Bay at South Seaside Park, turning north along current day Route 35 up to Bay Head. Vacationers began to flock to Lavallette by the turn of the century. The business district was established along Grand Central Avenue shortly after. The largest population growth was between 1940 and 1960, with the construction of the Rt. 37/Mathis Bridge and the opening of the Garden State Parkway. Today, Lavallette is the perfect family resort, clean, quiet, full of shops and restaurants, and close enough to the amusement boardwalks of Point Pleasant Beach to the north and Seaside Heights to the south.

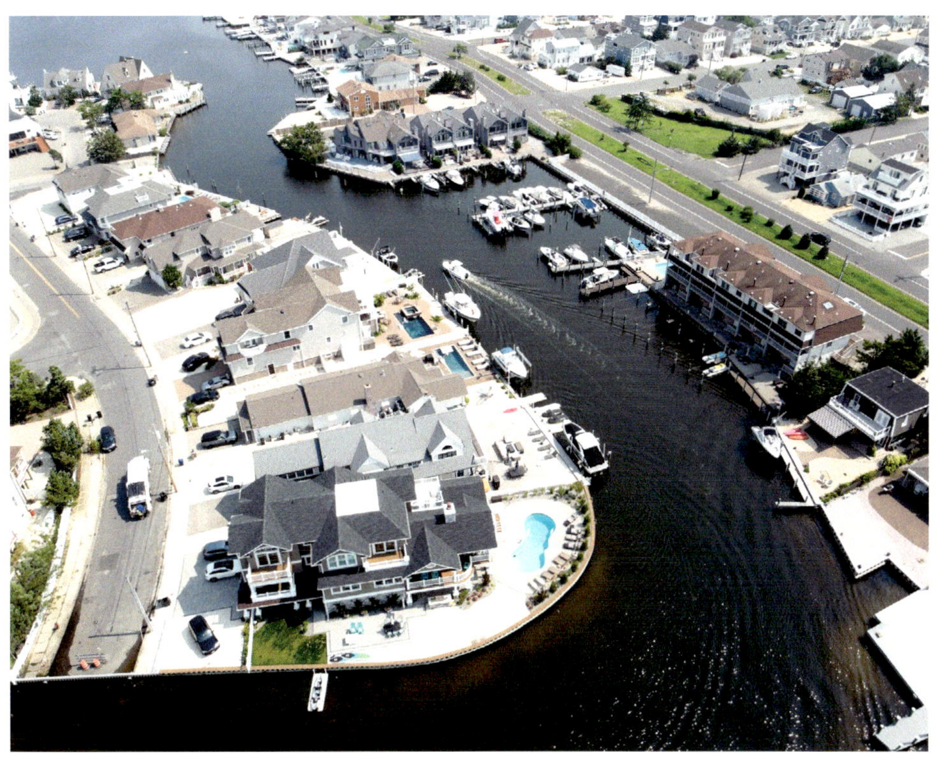

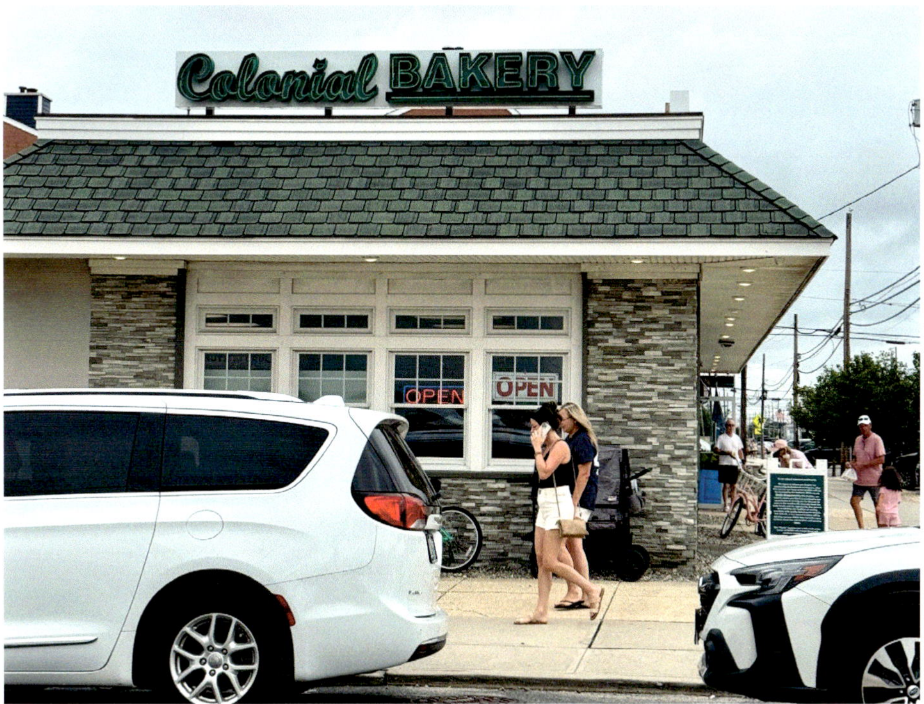

Colonial BAKERY
OPEN
OPEN

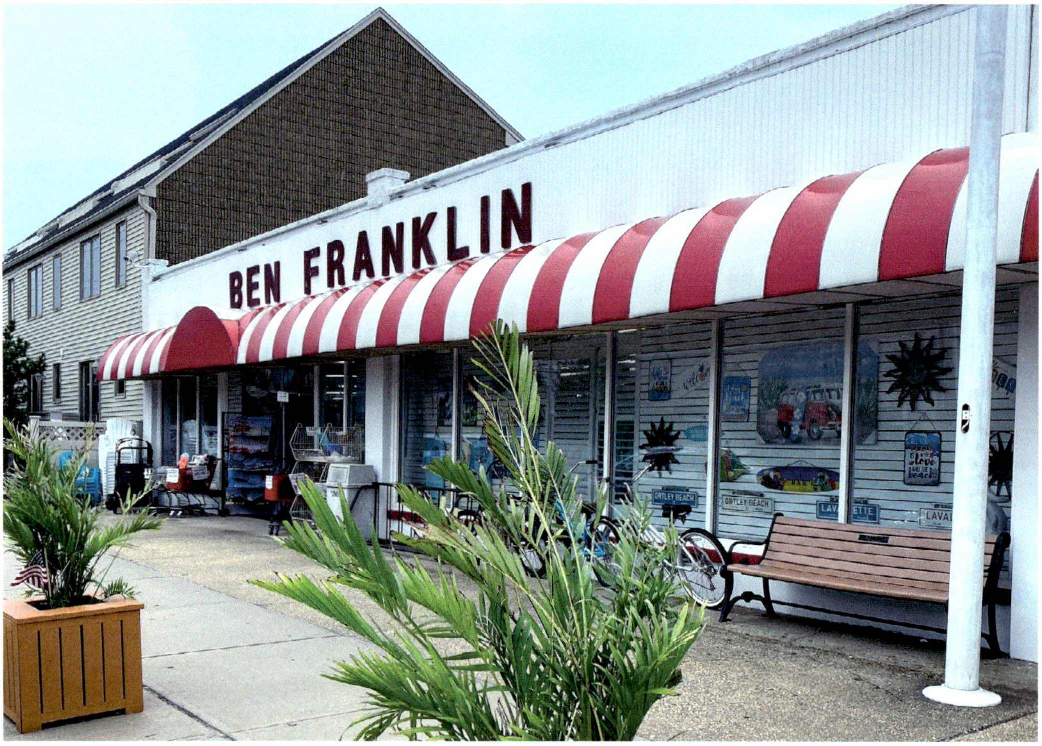

BEN FRANKLIN
ORTLEY BEACH
ORTLEY BEACH
LAVALLETTE
LAVAL

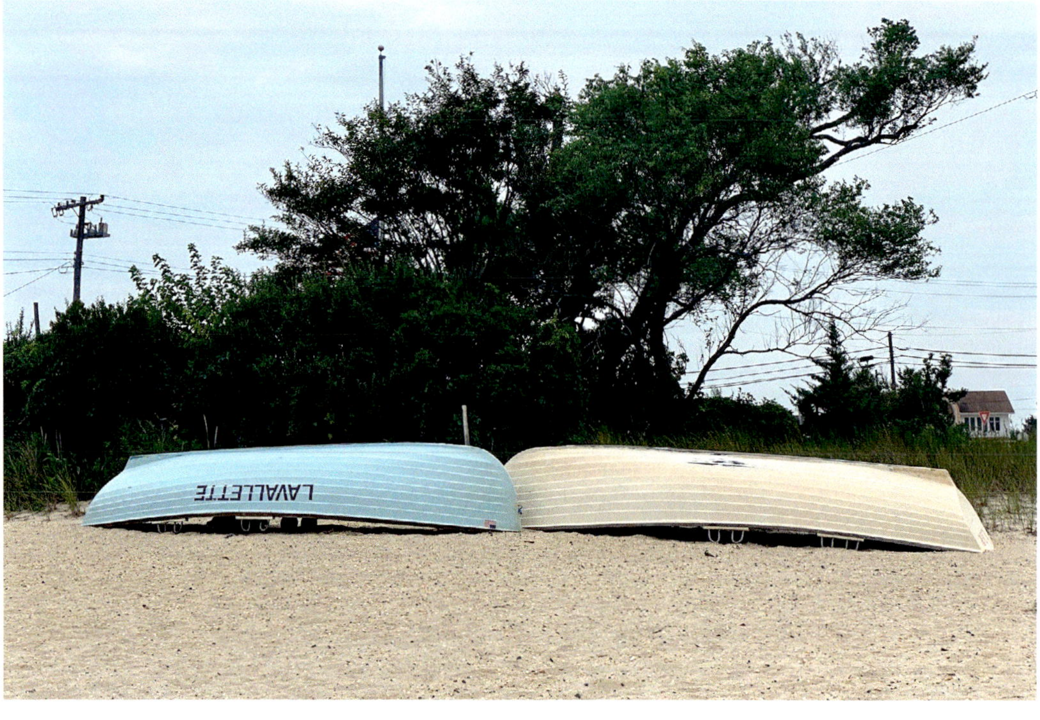

LAVALLETTE

DOVER BEACHES SOUTH (TOMS RIVER): ORTLEY BEACH

Incorporated: 1798
Motto: None
Origin of the name: Named after Michael Ortley
Formed from: Portions of Shrewsbury Township
Previous names: Cranberry Inlet

Situated at the midway point of the Barnegat Peninsula is Ortley Beach, the only town included in the Dover Beaches "South" designation. In the late 1700s, Cranberry Inlet connected the ocean with the bay, near the present-day Seaside-Ortley border. Land to the south of the inlet was known as Island Beach, while the upper part was called Squan Beach. After sandbars closed the inlet in 1812, landowner Michael Ortley rallied residents and fishermen to help reopen it. They were successful in 1821, but it closed up less than twenty-four hours later. The town was decimated in 2012, when Ortley Beach took a direct hit from Hurricane Sandy. More than 2,500 of the 2,600 houses in the town were damaged, while 200 homes were completely washed away. Like most of the Jersey Shore, Ortley rebuilt; however, the small bungalows that were once part of the town's charm gave way too much bigger houses, appearing even larger on their 13-foot pilings to prevent future flood damage. One of Ortley's many losses from the storm was Joey Harrison's Surf Club, which opened in 1973 as a beachfront venue with live music, DJs, teen nights, and an oceanfront bar. It stood on the site occupied by previous beach bars since the 1930s.

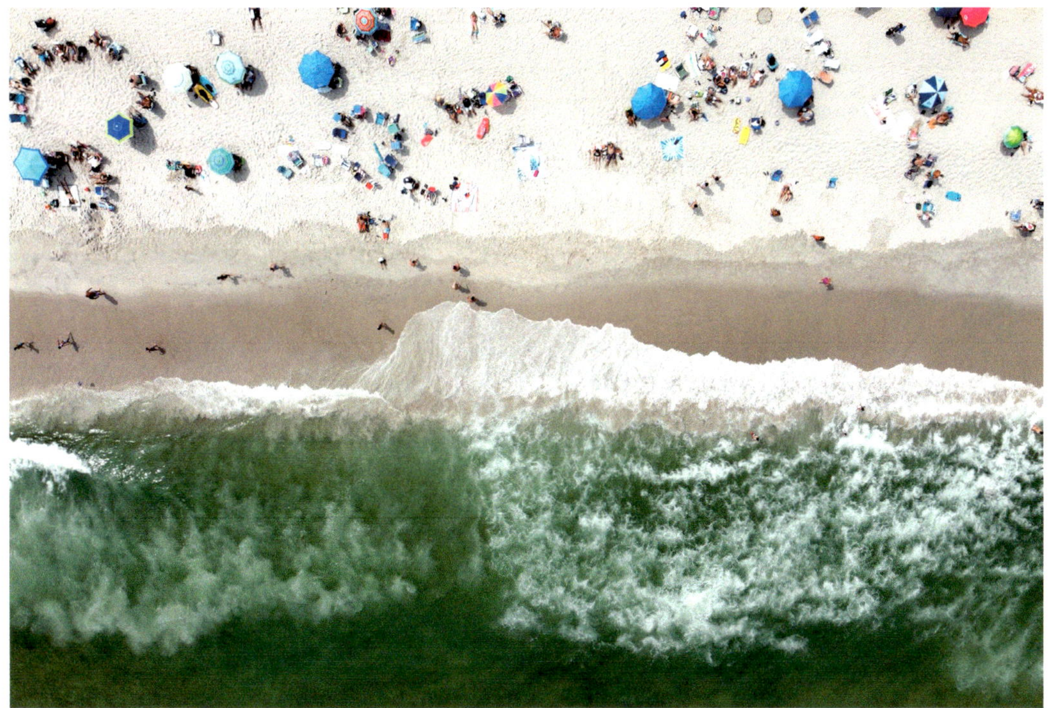

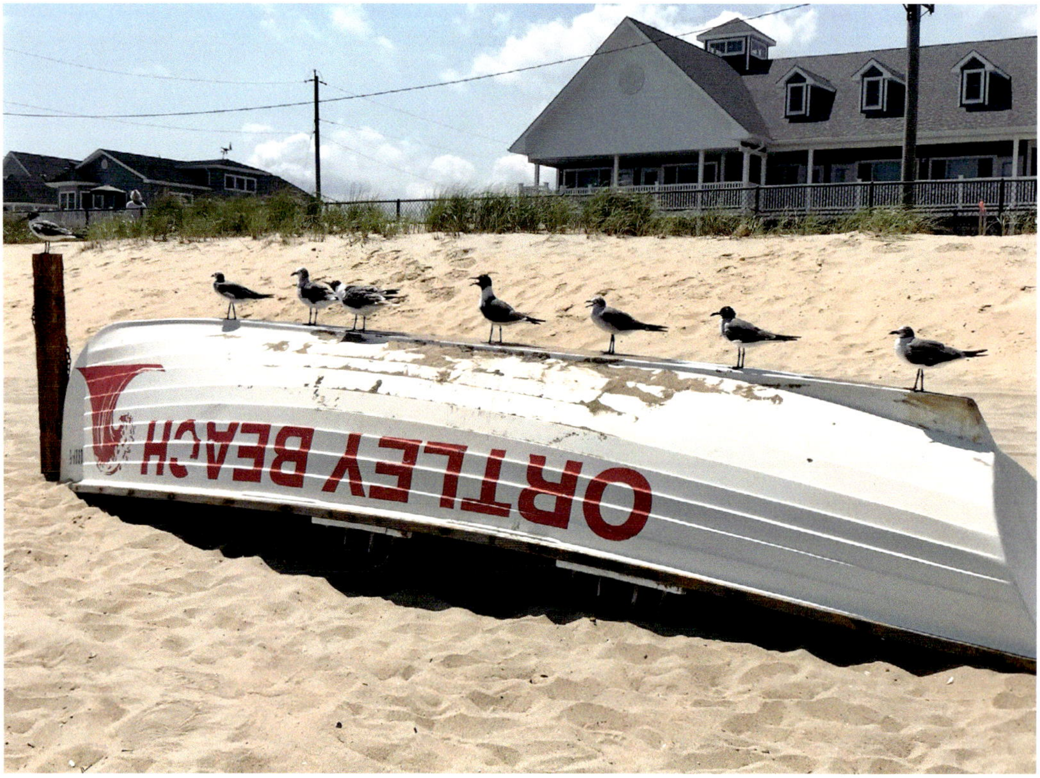

ORTLEY BEACH

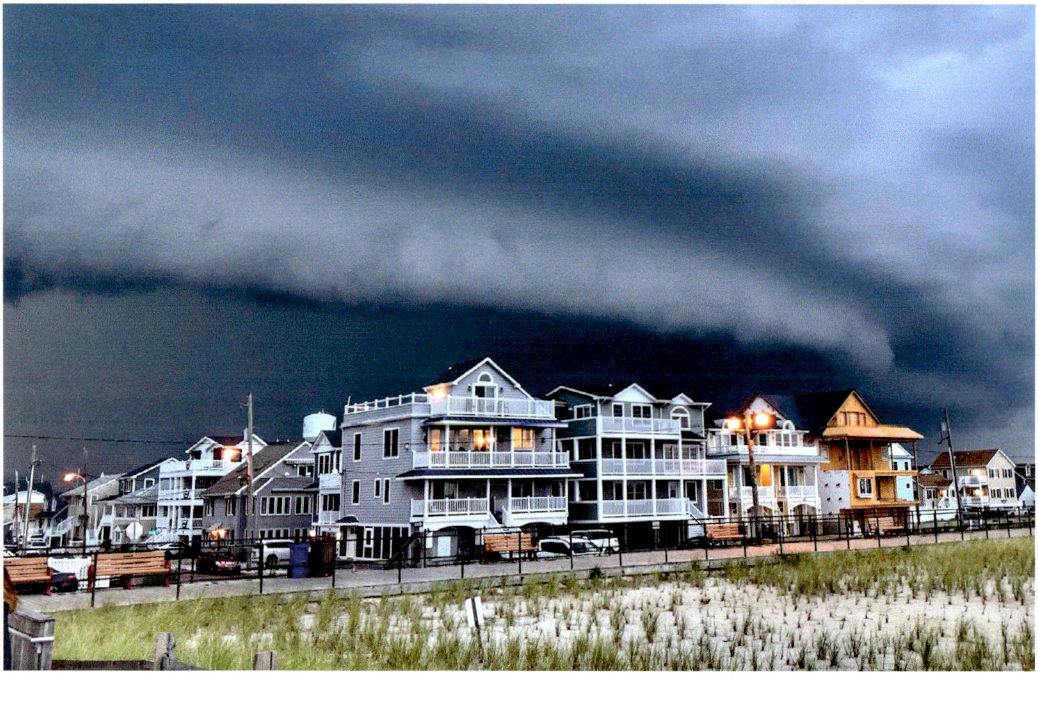

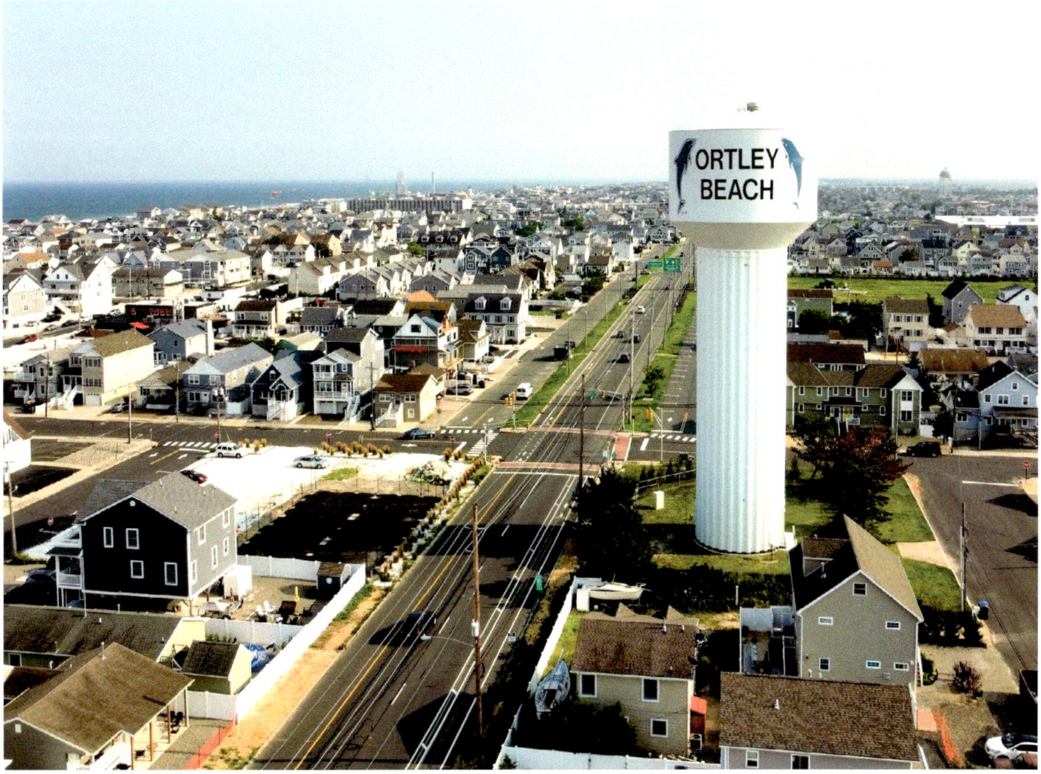

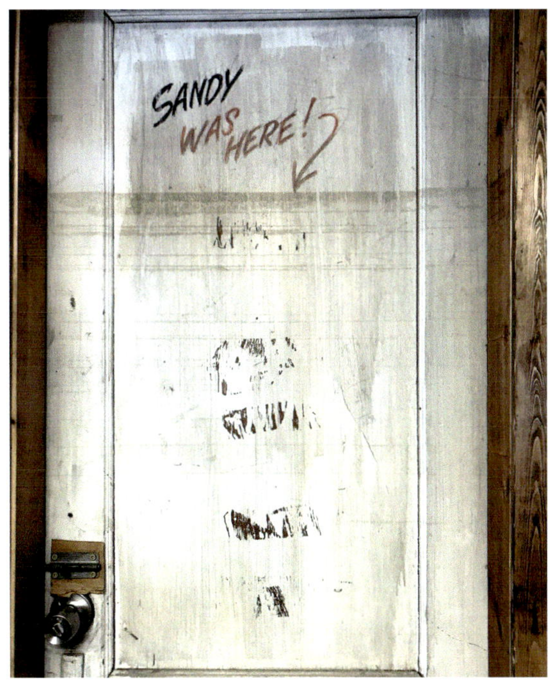
SANDY
WAS HERE!

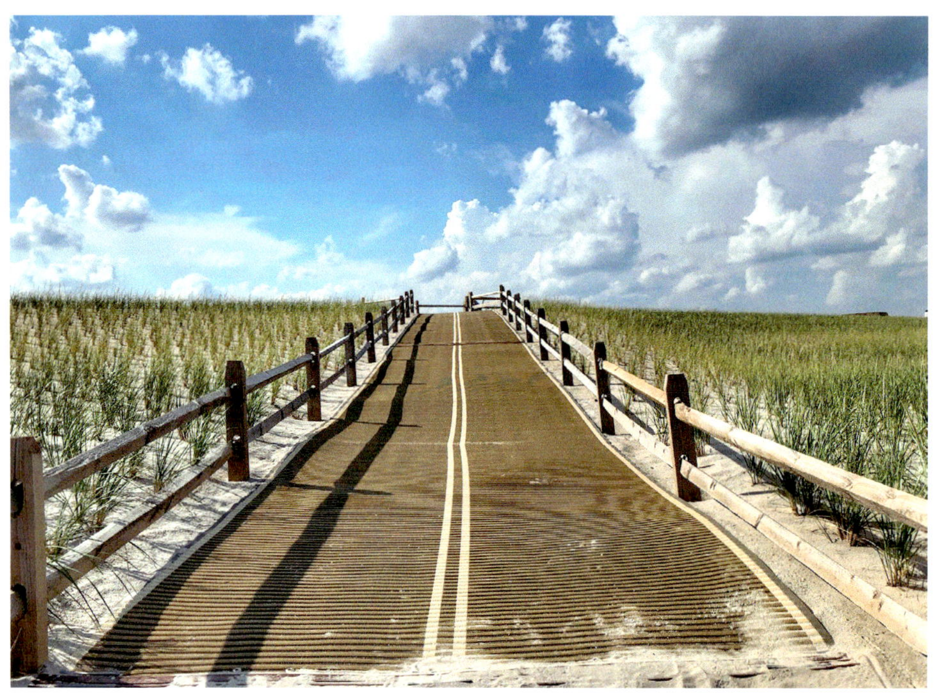

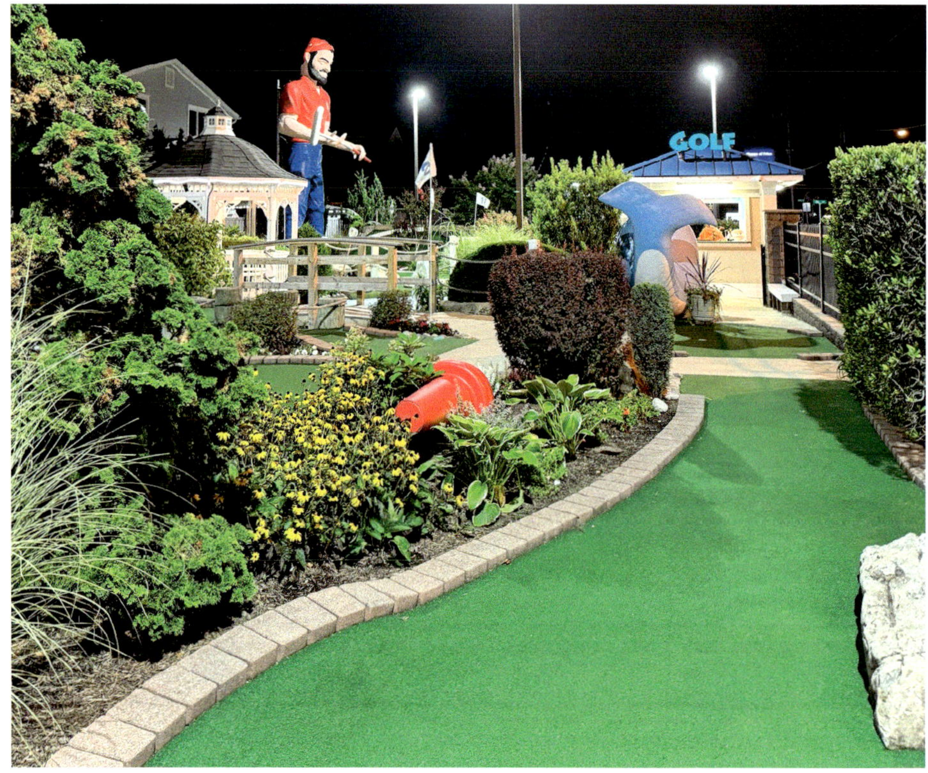

SEASIDE HEIGHTS

Incorporated: 1913
Motto: "Your Home for Family Fun Since 1913"
Origin of the name: Named for its location on the Atlantic Ocean
Formed from: Portions of Berkeley Township
Previous names: None

Due to the success of Seaside Park to the south, founded fifteen years earlier, a realty group set out to develop land to the north, which they called Seaside Heights. Soon after the completion of the Toms River Bridge in 1914, plans were made to add attractions to the new town; a carousel, boardwalk, and covered pier were built between 1915 and 1916. Over the next several decades, the boardwalk was extended north towards Ortley Beach, more pavilions and carousels were added, and the population began to boom. By the 1960s and '70s, the Seaside boardwalk was in full swing, attracting thousands of visitors every summer. The town was thrust into the national spotlight in 2009, when MTV aired season one of the *Jersey Shore*. Some of Seaside's most famous attractions are Midway Steaks, Casino Pier, Kohr's Frozen Custard, the Sawmill, the *Jersey Shore* house, and Lucky Leo's Arcade. Many will remember the haunting image of the Jet Star rollercoaster sitting in the ocean alongside the pier, another casualty of Hurricane Sandy. Some of the author's friends and family are pictured here enjoying another great August night on the Seaside boards.

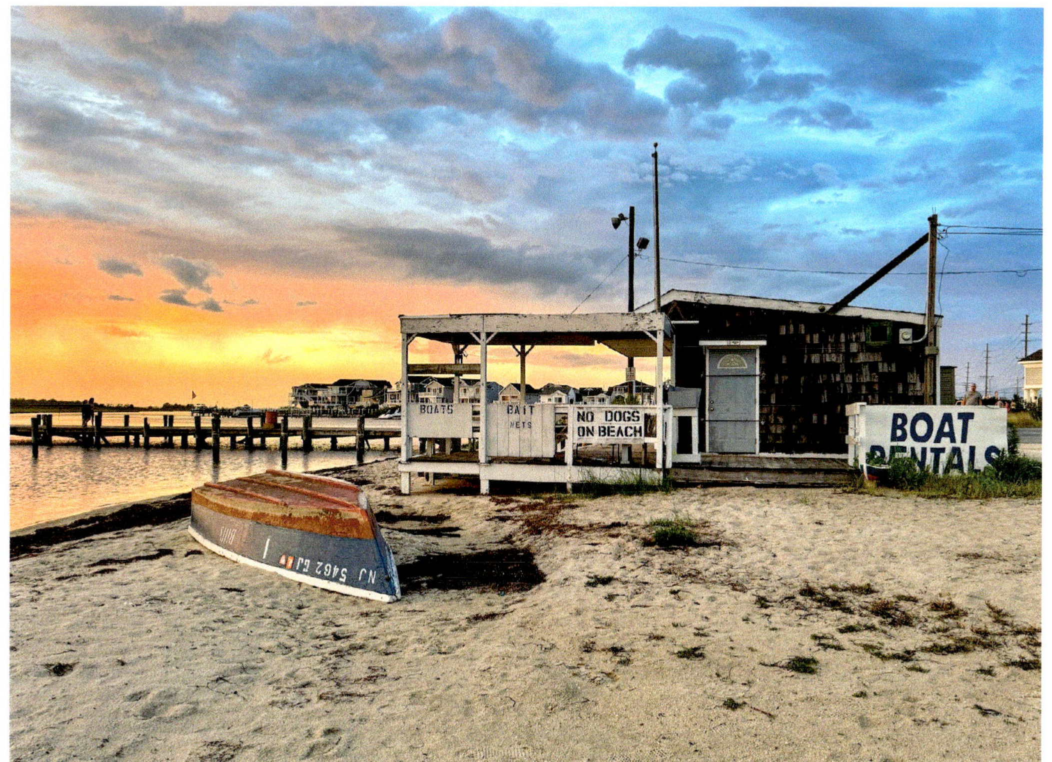

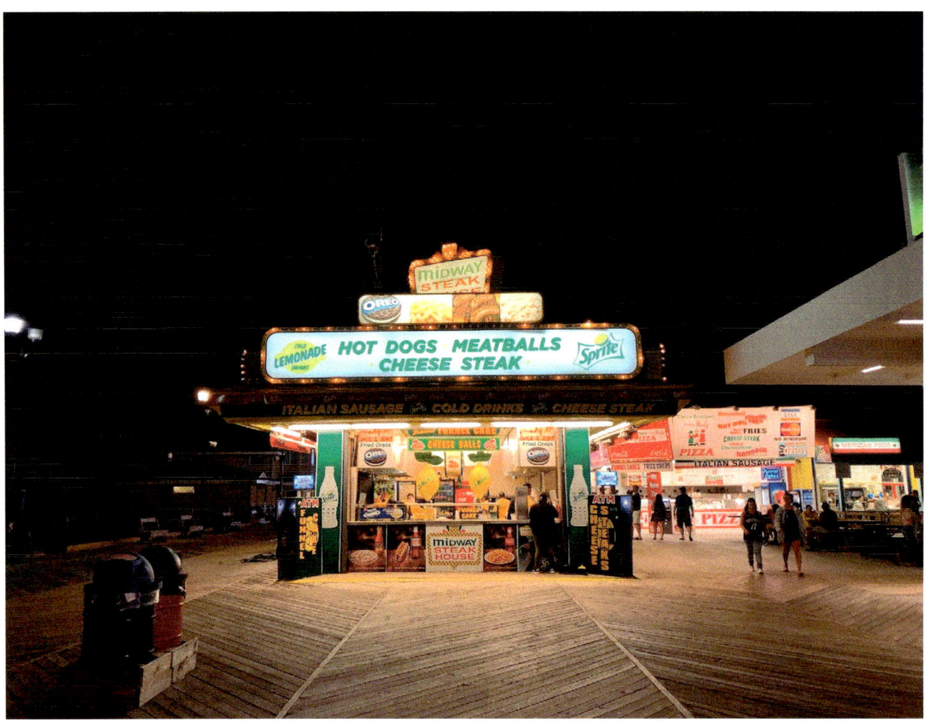
MIDWAY STEAK
OREO
LEMONADE DRINKS HOT DOGS MEATBALLS Sprite
CHEESE STEAK
ITALIAN SAUSAGE COLD DRINKS CHEESE STEAK
CHEESE BALLS
midway
STEAK
HOUSE
ATM
PIZZA
ITALIAN SAUSAGE
FRIES
CHEESE STEAK
PIZZA
MEXICAN FOOD

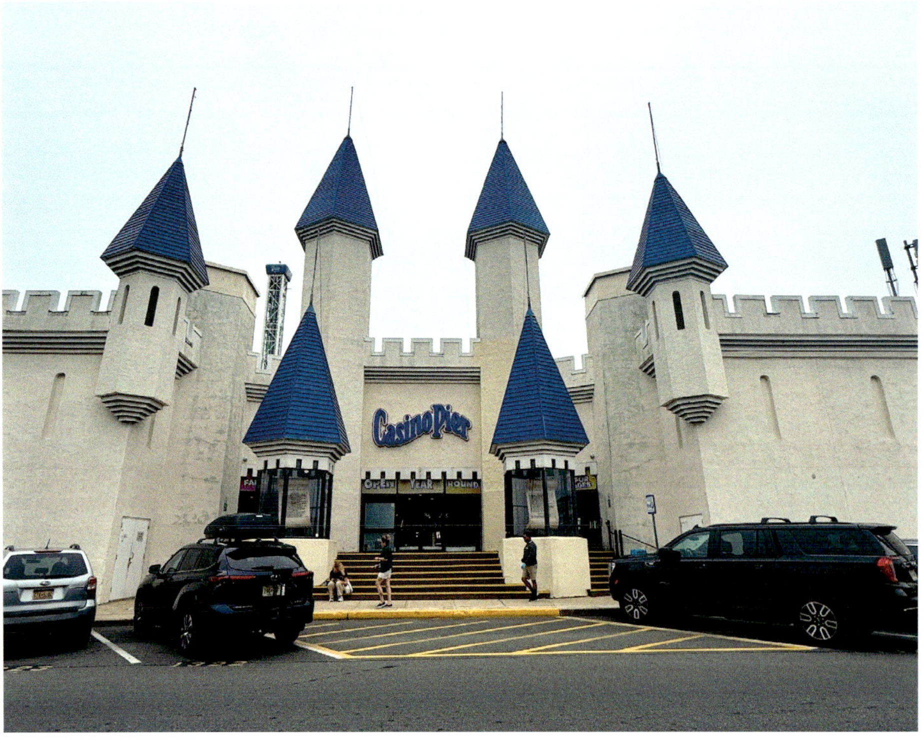
Casino Pier
OPEN YEAR ROUND

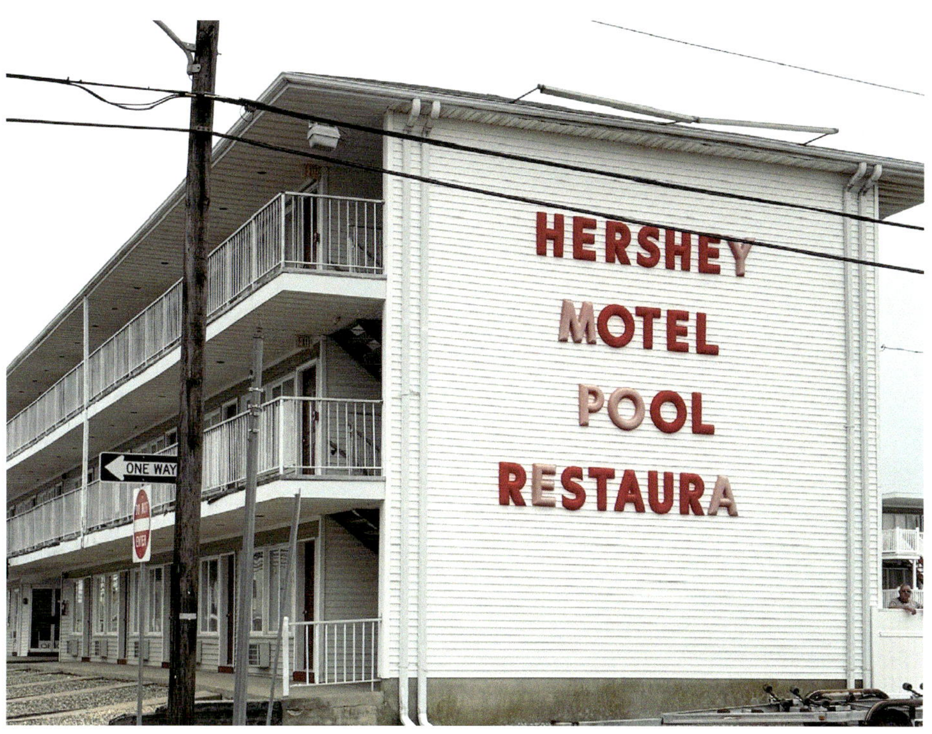

HERSHEY
MOTEL
POOL
RESTAURA
ONE WAY

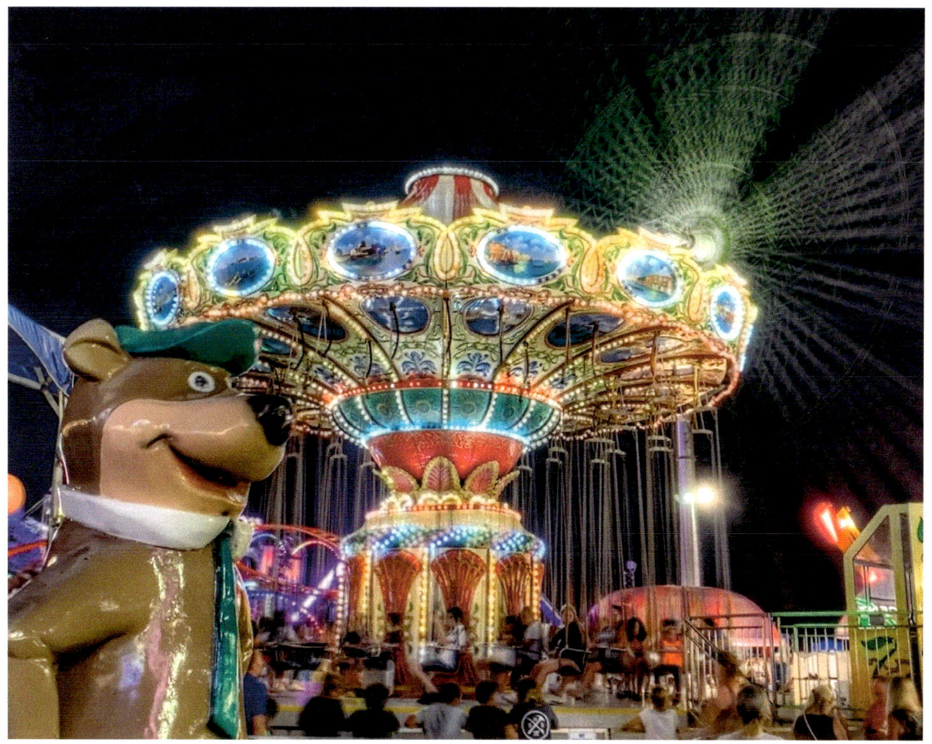

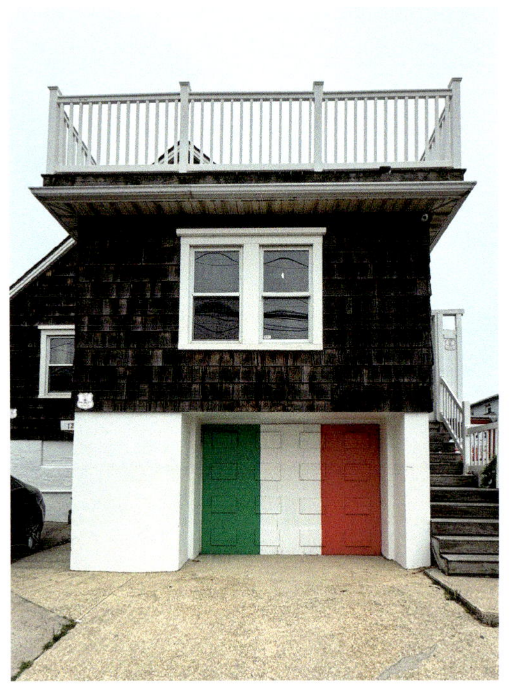

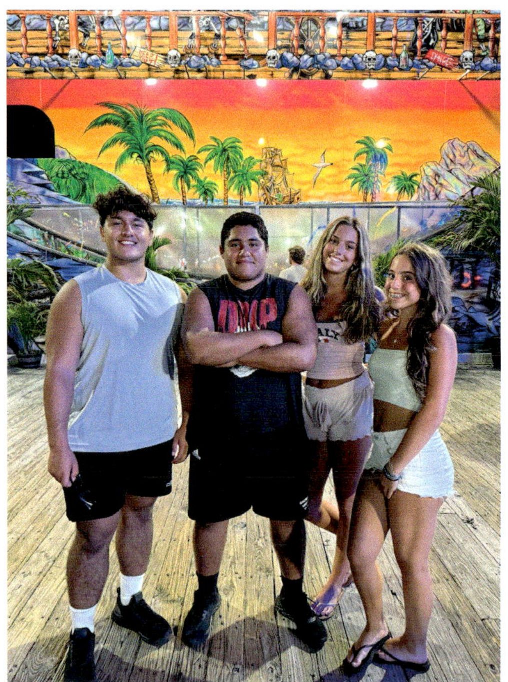

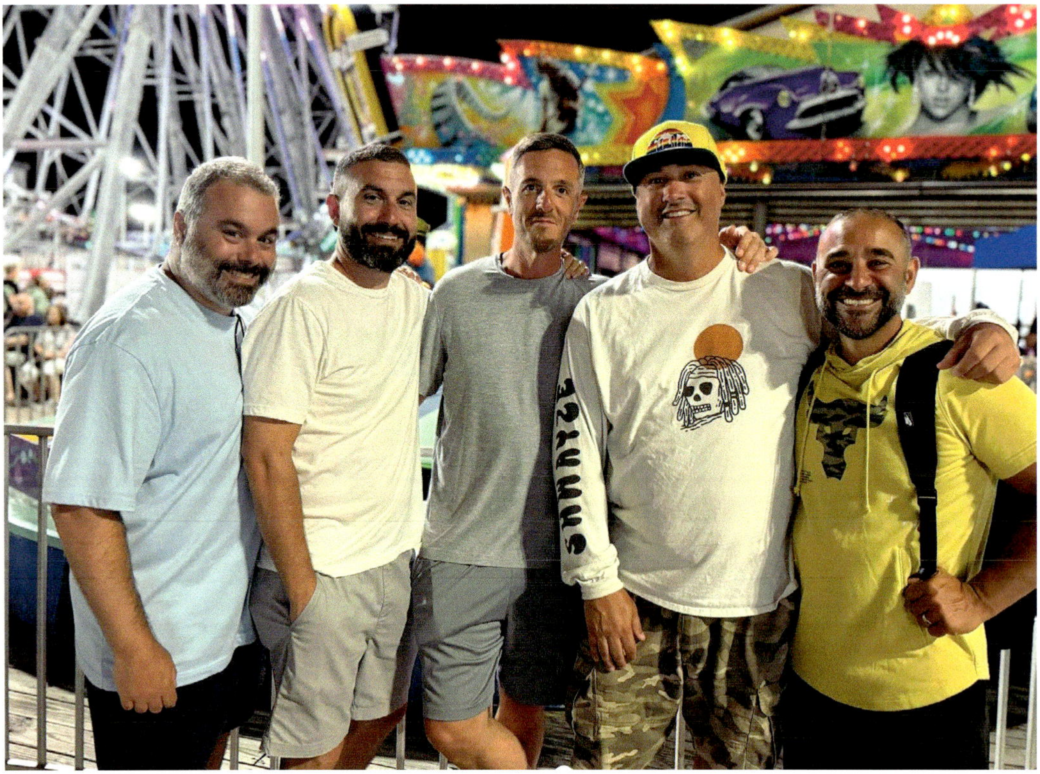

SEASIDE PARK

Incorporated:	1898
Motto:	"The Family Resort"
Origin of the name:	Named for its location on the Atlantic Ocean
Formed from:	Portions of Berkeley Township
Previous names:	Park City, Sea Side Park, Seheyichbi, the Lenape word for "land bordering the ocean"

The area now known as Seaside Park was originally part of Dover Township until Berkeley Township was created in 1875, when it became known as the "Sea Side Park" section of Berkeley Township. As roads were built throughout the community, more lots were sold, houses were constructed, and the town began to grow. In 1898, it was incorporated as its own borough, but didn't reach its current size until the Berkeley Tract to the north was annexed in 1900. South Seaside Park remains part of Berkeley Township. Due to a clerical error in 1914, the borough was recorded as "Seaside Park," and the name has stuck ever since. Much of the Seaside Park and bordering Seaside Heights boardwalk were destroyed by a devastating fire in 2013, where sustained winds helped the fire spread and destroy more than fifty businesses, including the Funtown Pier.

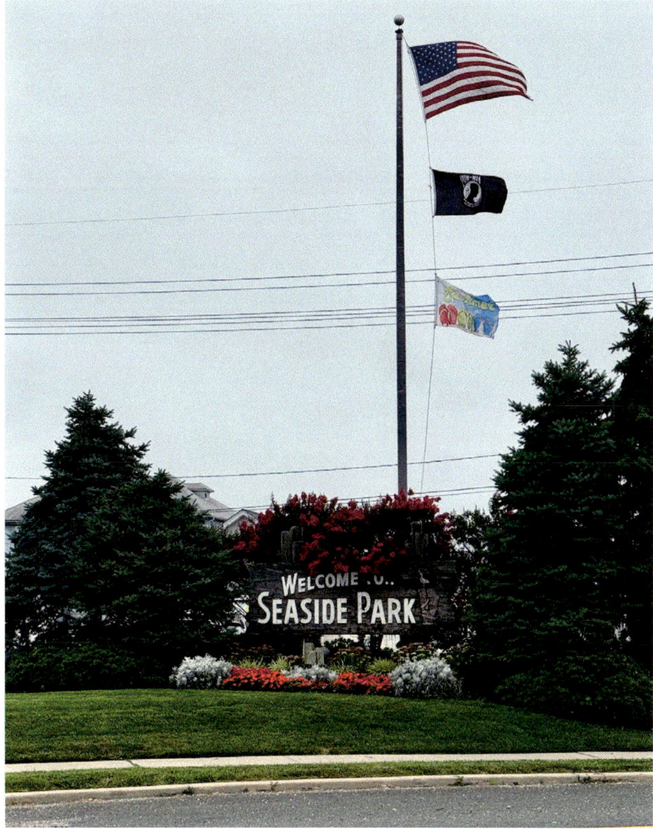

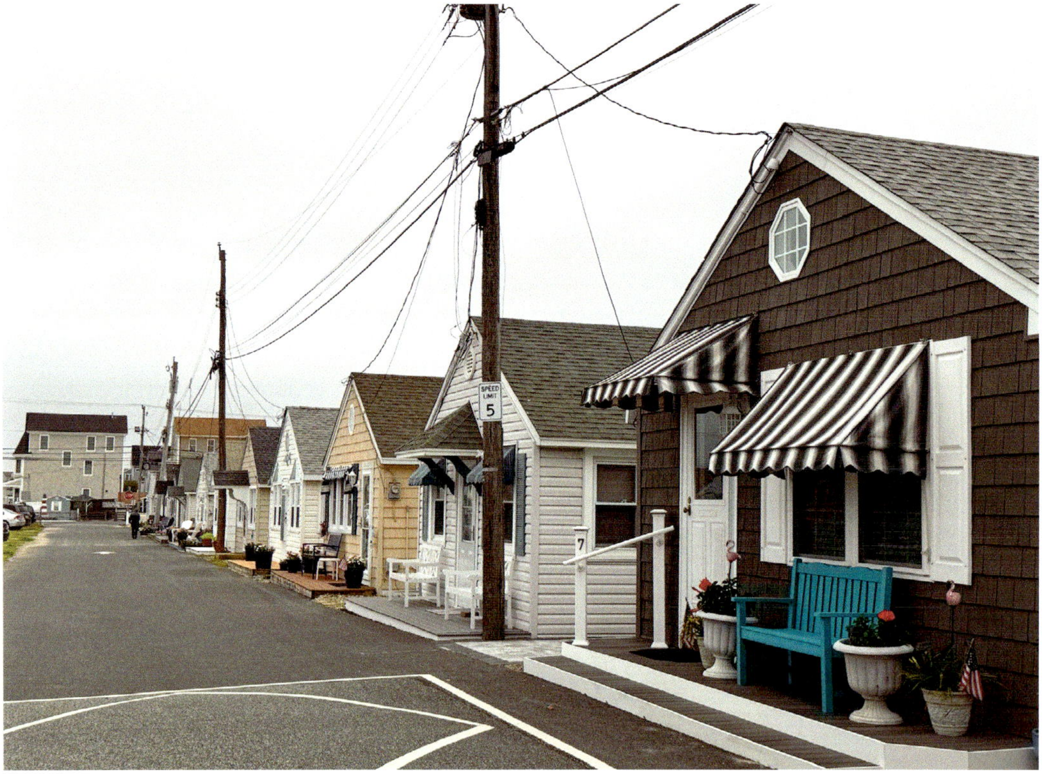

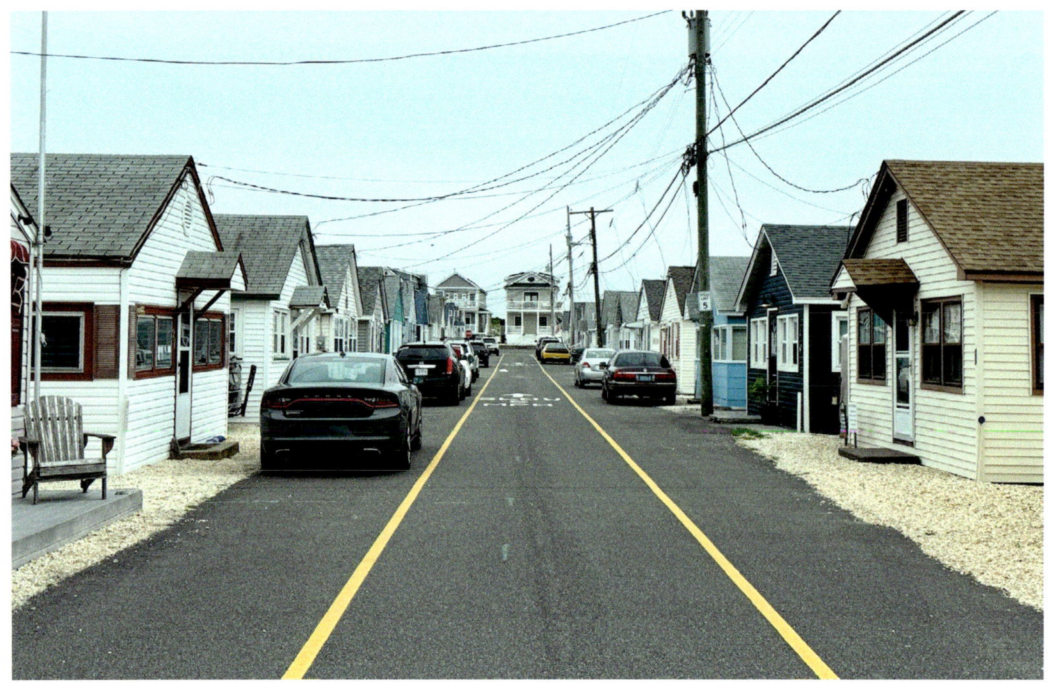

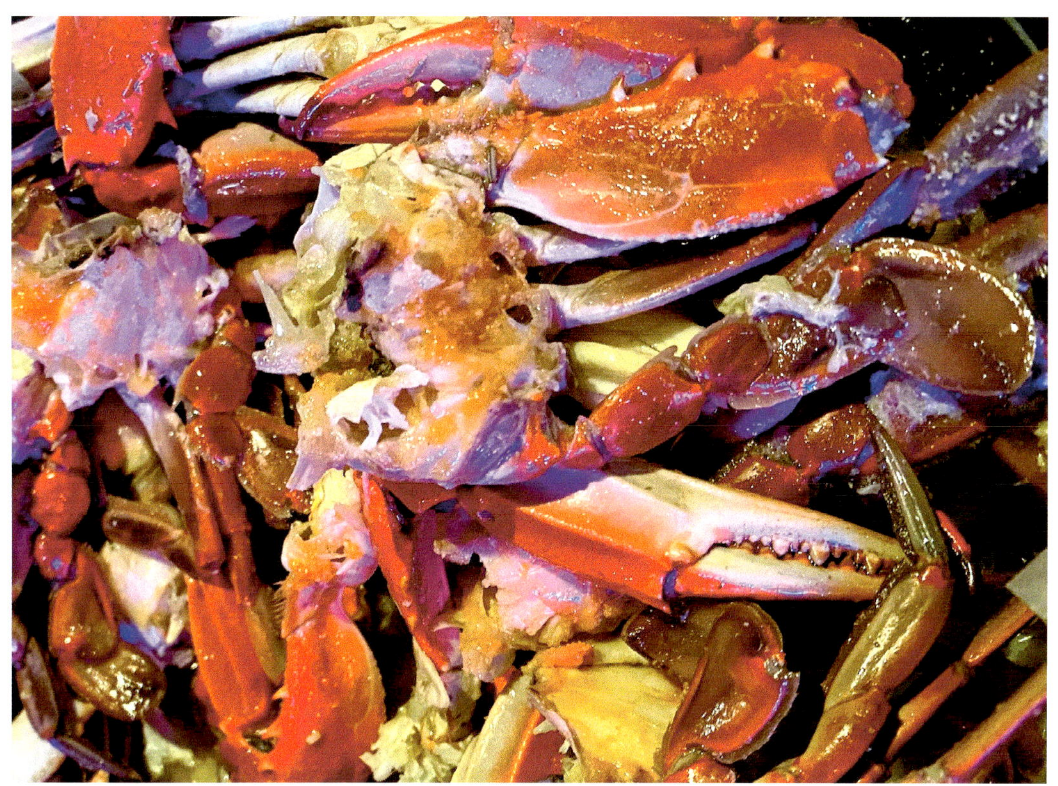

ISLAND BEACH STATE PARK

Established: 1953; opened to the public in 1959
Motto: None
Origin of the name: Named for its location on the Atlantic Ocean
Formed from: Portions of Berkeley Township
Previous names: Borough of Island Beach

Tracing back hundreds of years, Island Beach has always been a fisherman's paradise. First, for the Lenape, followed by English settlers who built small, wooden fishing shacks, and continuing to this day for anglers all over the state, looking to land a "cow" striper and other species. In 1926, Henry Phipps, one of Andrew Carnegie's partners, purchased the land and established it as the Borough of Island Beach. The state acquired the Phipps estate in 1953 to preserve the land, and maintain its natural beauty, which consists of maritime forests, sandy dunes, estuaries, an oceanside beach, and a bay access. While most of Island Beach is undeveloped, there are several buildings of note, including the "Judge's Shack" (1911); the summer home/fishing "shack" of Judge Richard Hartshorne, and the Governor's Summer Mansion, formerly the Phipps summer home.

The southern tip of Island Beach State Park ends at the Barnegat Inlet, which separates the Barnegat Peninsula from Long Beach Island.

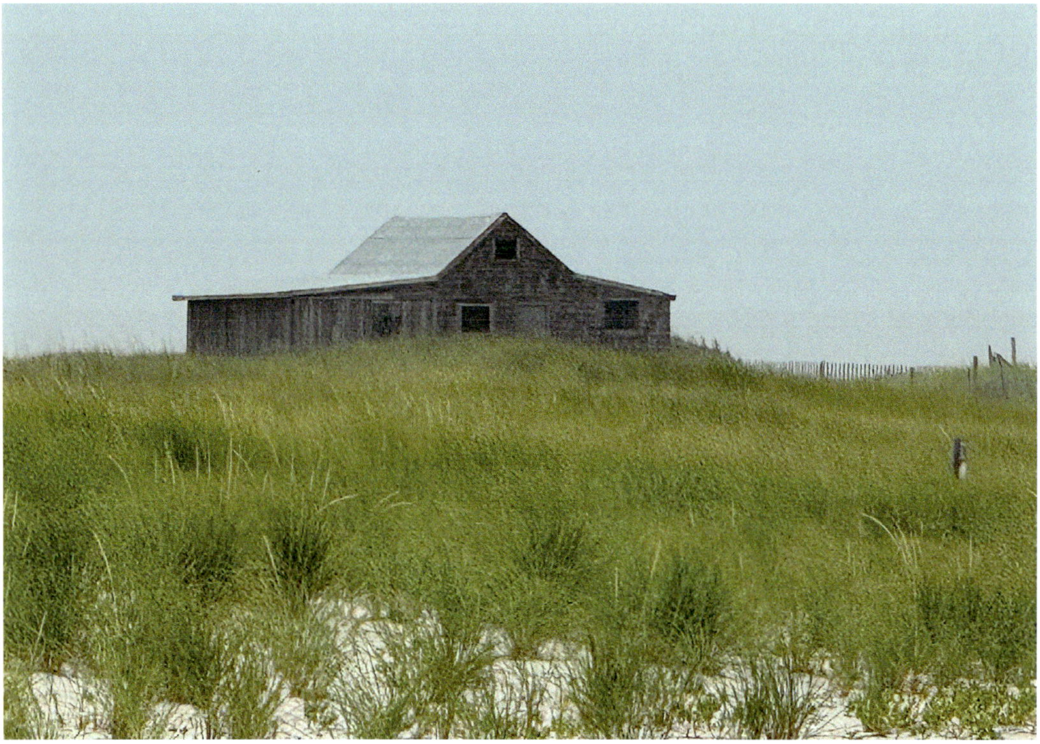

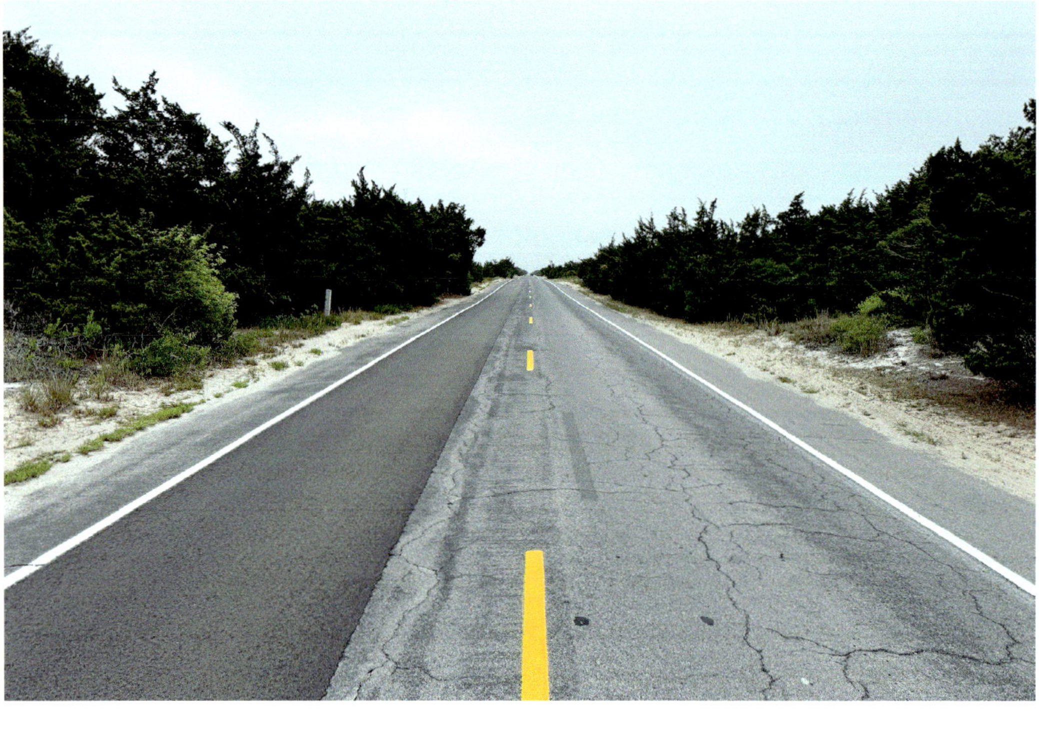

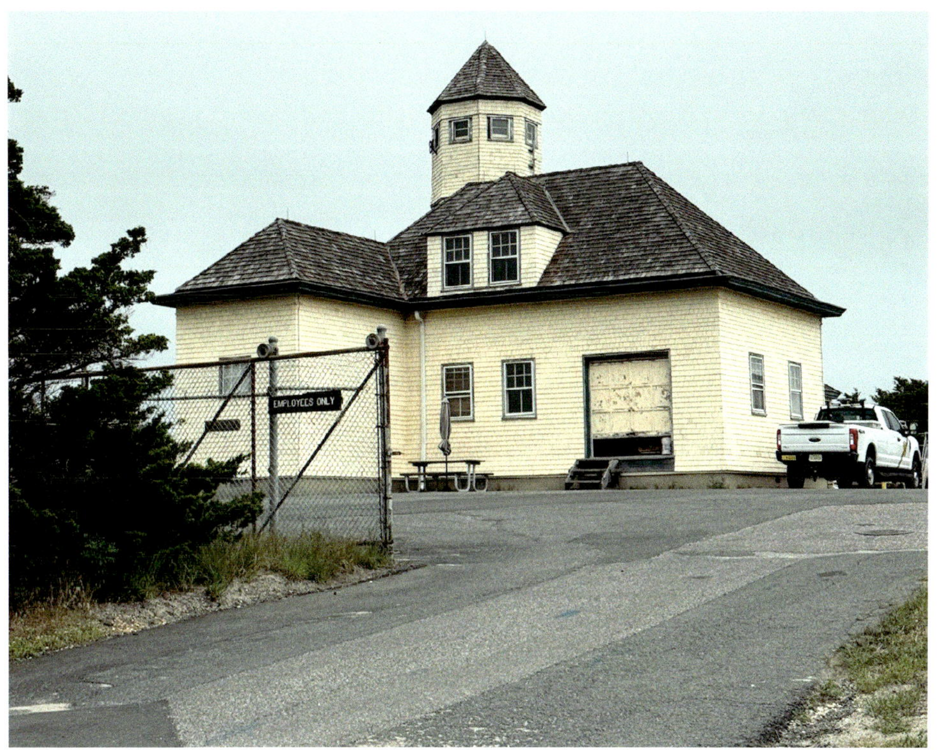

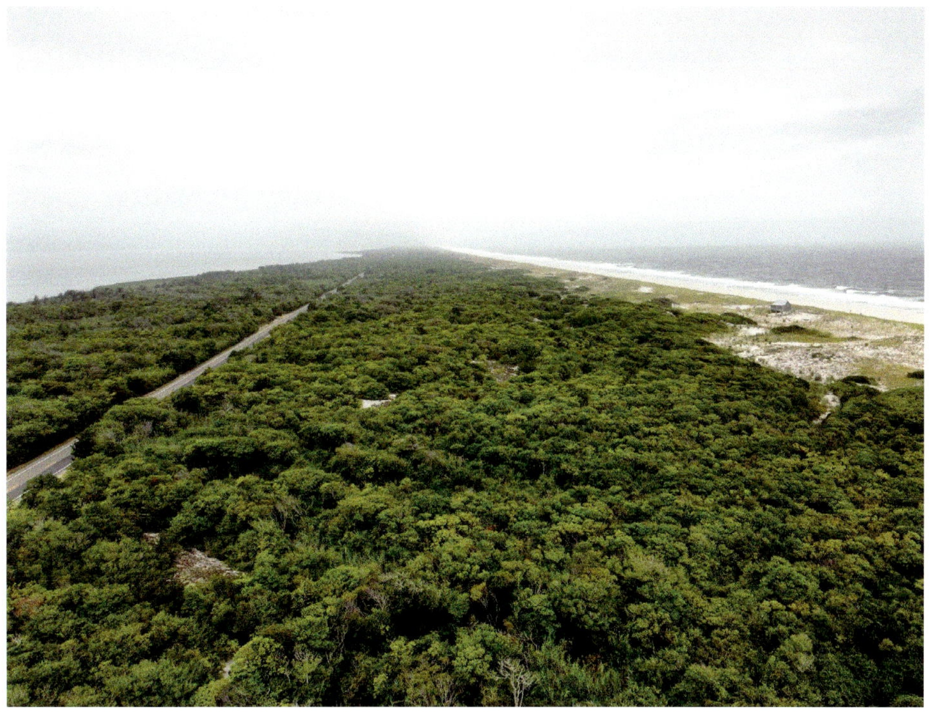

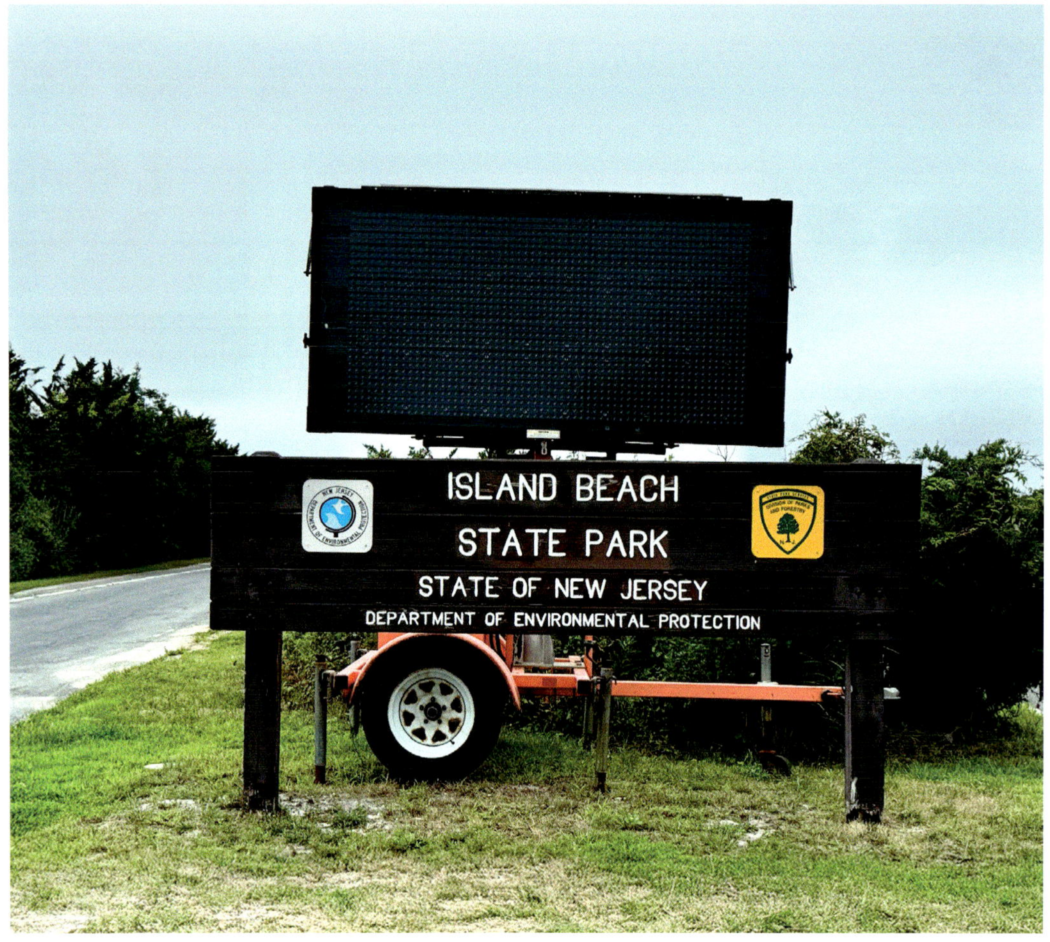

LONG BEACH ISLAND

Long Beach Island stretches for 18 miles and is comprised of more than twenty different towns, divided into six non-contiguous townships: Barnegat Light, Harvey Cedars, Surf City, Ship Bottom, Beach Haven, and Long Beach Township. Long Beach Township contains the following neighborhoods and communities: Bay Vista, Beach Haven Crest, Beach Haven Gardens, Beach Haven Heights, Beach Haven Inlet, Beach Haven Park, Beach Haven Terrace, Brighton Beach, Haven Beach, High Bar Harbor, Brant Beach, Loveladies, North Beach, North Beach Haven, Peahala Park, South Beach Haven, Spray Beach, the Dunes, and Holgate.

BARNEGAT LIGHT

Incorporated:	1904 as Barnegat City; renamed in 1948 as Barnegat Light
Motto:	None
Origin of the name:	"Barende-gat," from the Dutch word for "Breakers Inlet"
Formed from:	Portions of Berkeley Township
Previous names:	Barnegat Beach, Brownsville, Barnegat City

Early settlers referred to the area as Barnegat Beach, the oceanside neighbor to the mainland town of Barnegat on the other side of the bay. In 1834, the first lighthouse on the island was built to help vessels navigate the inlet, a major shipping channel for inland seaport towns like Tuckerton. A new lighthouse, now known as "Old Barney," would be commissioned in 1859, designed by U.S. Army engineer and future Civil War general George Meade. In the 1920s and '30s, storm damage, erosion, and the discontinuation of rail service led to the decline of the town, but efforts to protect the shorelines through a series of jetties helped reclaim land lost and re-establish the town as an attractive resort.

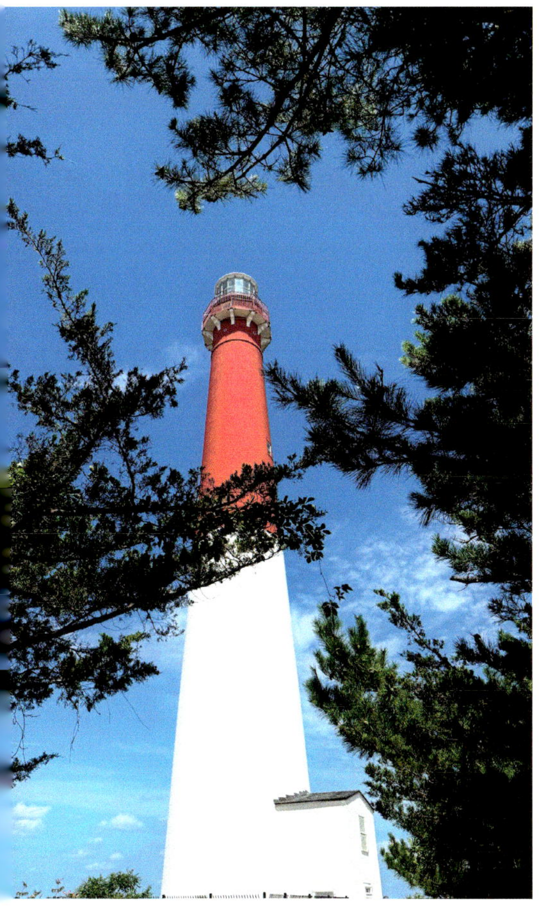

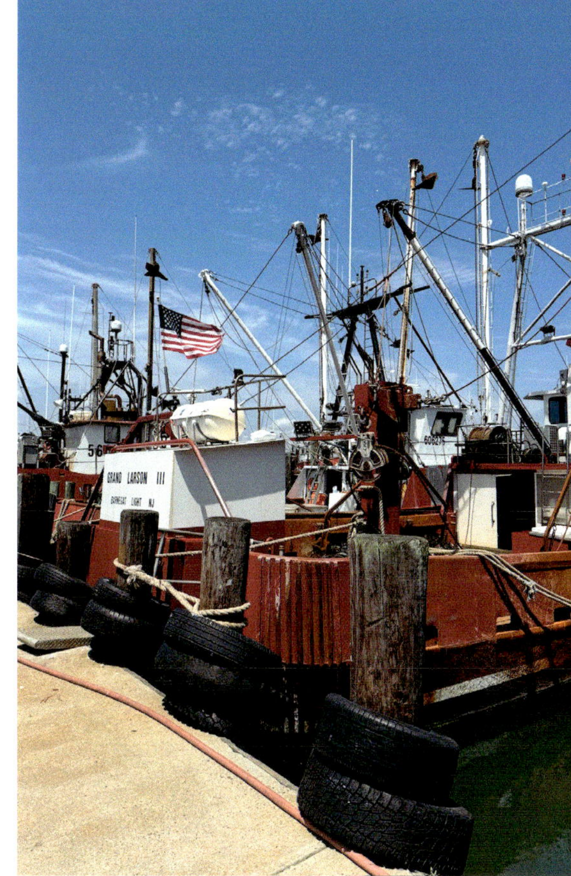

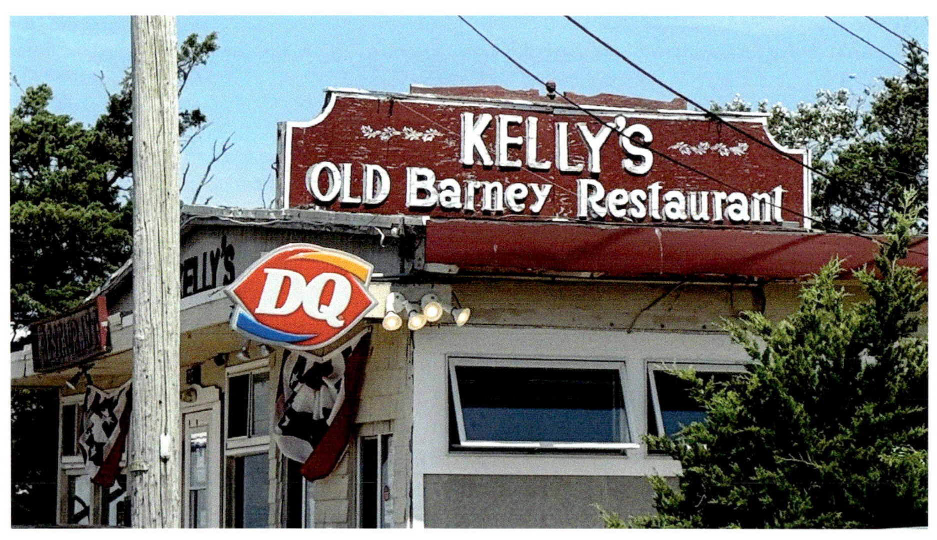

KELLY'S
OLD Barney Restaurant
KELLY'S
DQ

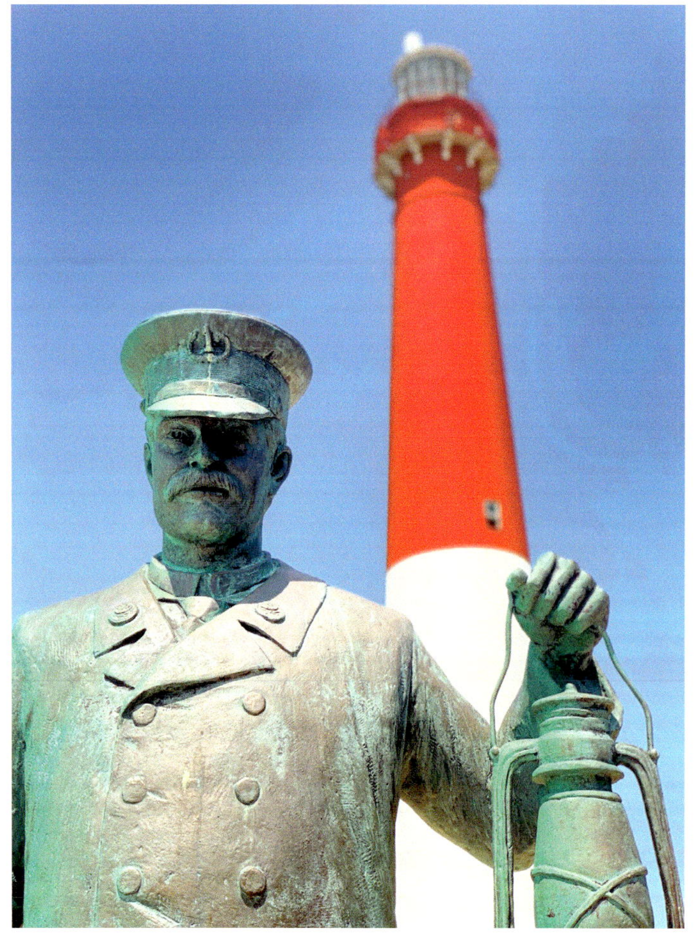

HARVEY CEDARS

Incorporated: 1894
Motto: None
Origin of the name: Derivation of Harvest Quarters
Formed from: Portions of Barnegat Township
Previous names: Harvest Quarters, High Point

Most of LBI was covered with American White Cedar prior to development. While some settlers in the area arrived to take part in the whaling industry, many others built shacks, or quarters, for eelgrass, seaweed, and salt hay harvesting. In 1886, the Harvey Cedars Beach Company mapped out the land for development. Around this time, life was centered around the lifesaving station (now the Fishing Club) and the Harvey Cedars Hotel (formerly Kinsey's, now the Bible Conference). Construction of the causeway, boulevard, and rail service to the area in the early part of the twentieth century led to a summer population boom. Much of the community was destroyed by hurricane in 1944, and then again in the Ash Wednesday nor'easter of 1962, dubbed "the Storm of the Century." Visitors today can enjoy a stroll through Sunset Park, dinner at Black-Eyed Susans or fresh seafood from the Harvey Cedars Shellfish Company.

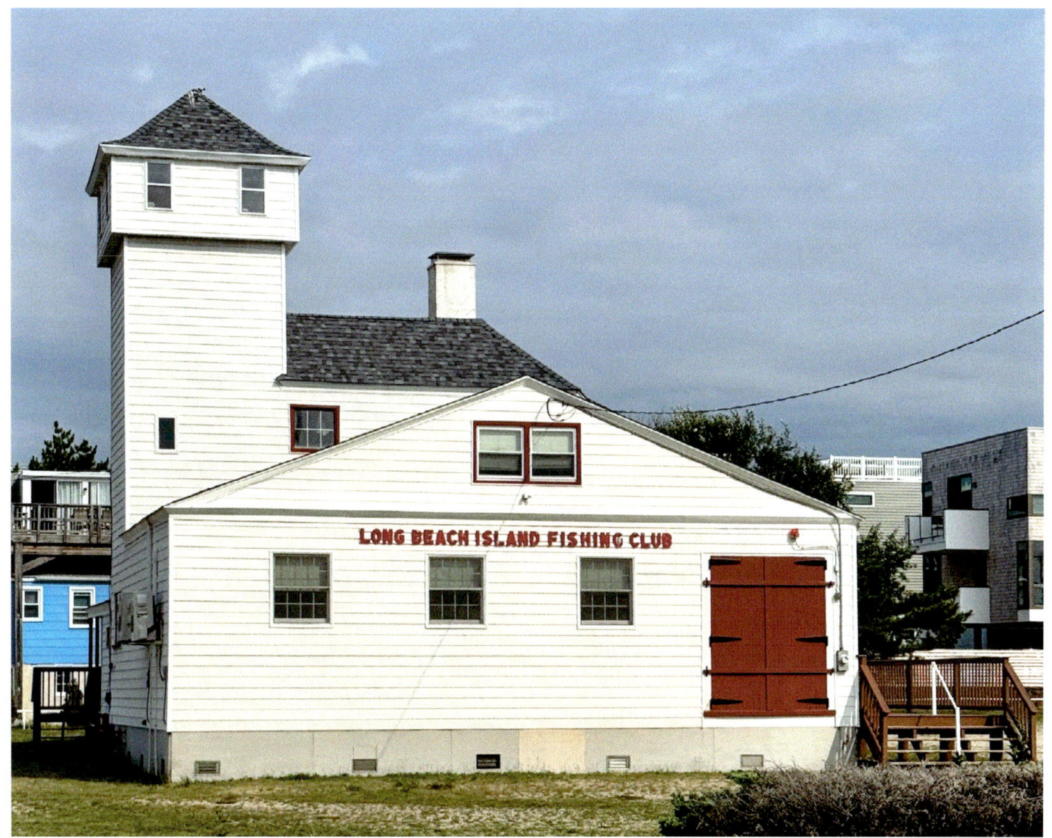

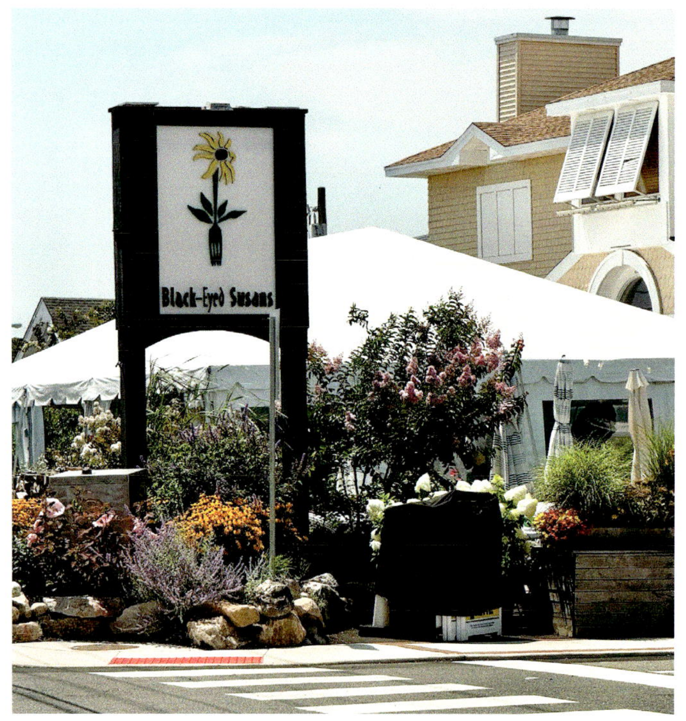
Black-Eyed Susans

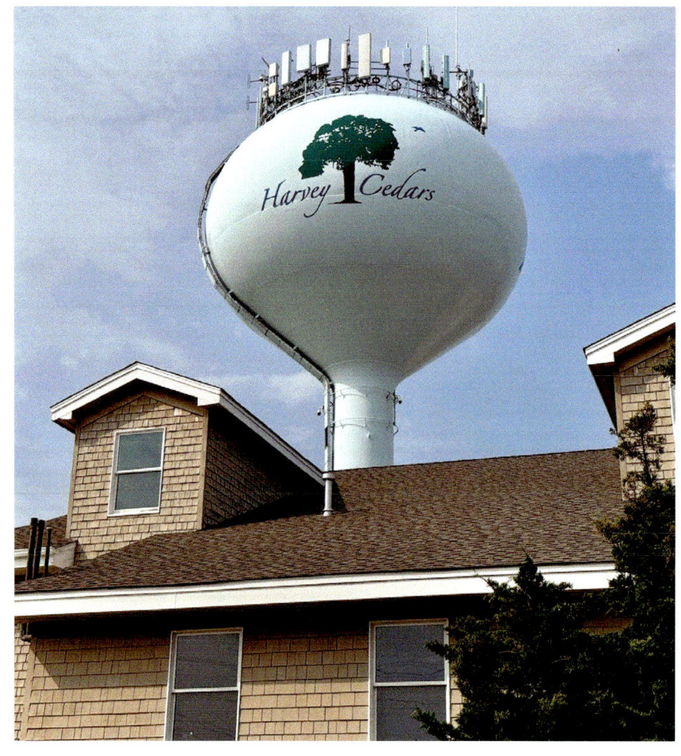
Harvey Cedars

SURF CITY

Incorporated:	1894 as Long Beach City, 1899 as Surf City
Motto:	None
Origin of the name:	Named for clean white surf at the shoreline
Formed from:	Portions of Stafford Township
Previous names:	the Great Swamp, Buzby's Place, Old Mansion, Long Beach City

The land where Surf City is located used to be a freshwater swamp with white cedar forests. Founded in 1690 as a whaling community, Surf City is LBI's oldest settlement. One of the oldest hotels/boarding houses on the Jersey Shore was the called the Mansion of Health, opened in Surf City in 1821, the same year a hurricane destroyed the swamp and forest with seawater. In the late 1800s, the Mansion House was constructed, changing its name to the Marquette Hotel and eventually the Surf City Hotel, which still stands today as a restaurant and place to stay. In 1899, the U.S. Post Office asked Long Beach City to change its name, so mail carriers would not confuse poorly written addresses with Long Branch City to the north. Town officials settled on Surf City. Harvey Cedars and Surf City would become known as art communities, with many eclectic shops and studios throughout.

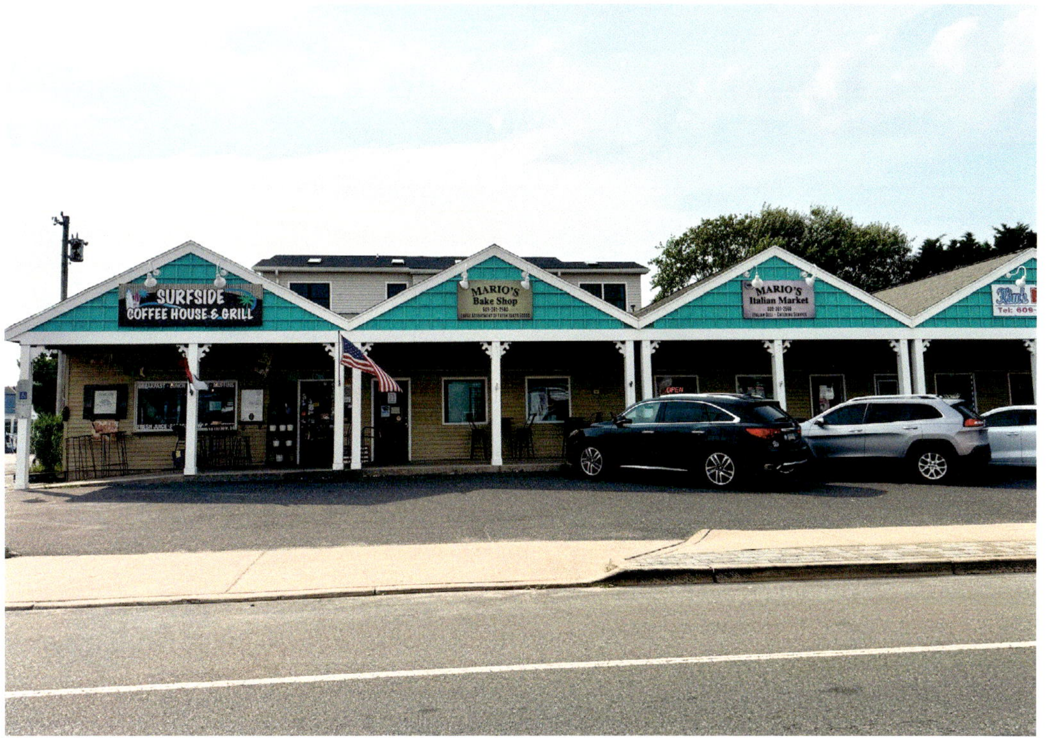

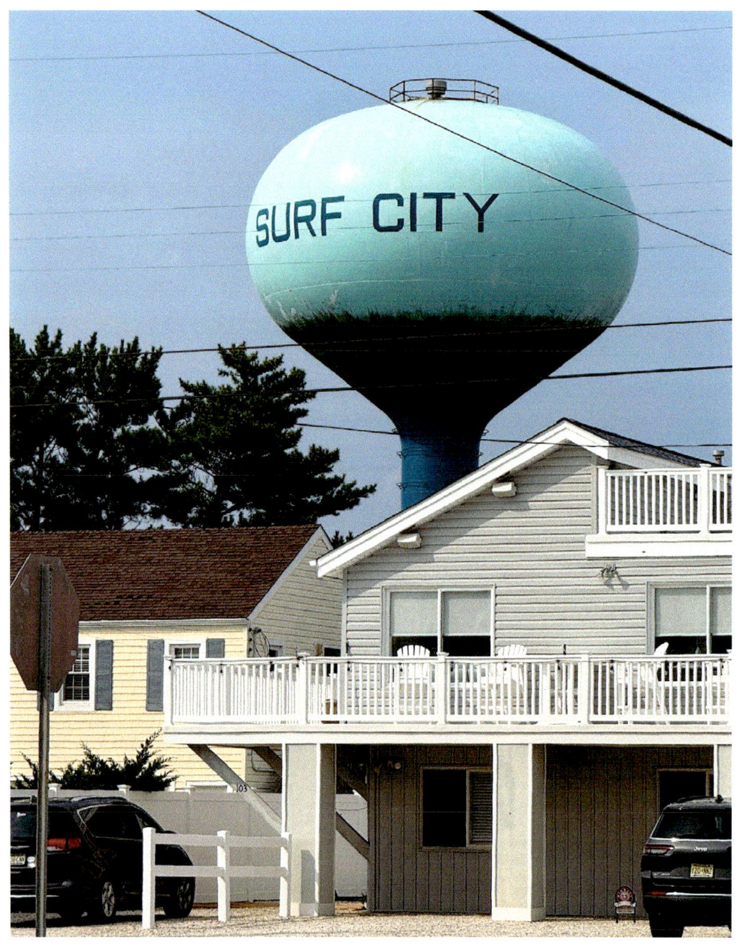

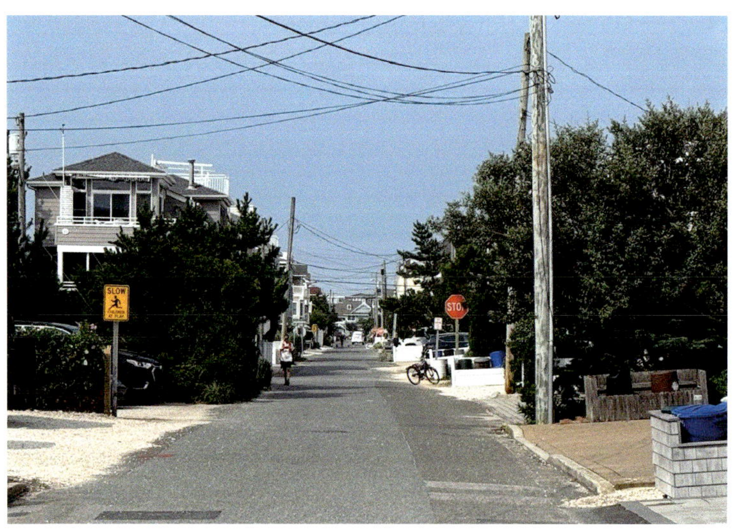

SHIP BOTTOM

Incorporated: 1925 as Ship Bottom-Beach Arlington, 1947 as Ship Bottom
Motto: "Gateway to Long Beach Island"
Origin of the name: Named after a historic rescue of a capsized ship in the area
Formed from: Portions of Long Beach Township
Previous names: Ship Bottom-Beach Arlington

The town's unique name was derived from a heroic rescue at sea in 1817, when a woman, trapped in the hull of a capsized ship, was saved when rescuers freed her by opening a hole in the bottom of the ship with axes. Almost a century later, the Italian ship *Fortuna* ran aground off the coast and rested on its side for several months. This led to the iconic Ship Bottom town logo/seal. At the turn of the century, there were only two or three houses in Ship Bottom, but more were built when rail service reached the area in 1914. The Causeway, connecting the mainland to LBI, opened in 1914, allowing vacationers to drive themselves to the island for the first time. No matter which LBI destination one is headed to, they must pass through Ship Bottom to get there. In 1925, the towns of Bonnie Beach, Bonnet Beach, Edgewater Beach, Beach Arlington, and Ship Bottom joined together to form the borough of Ship Bottom-Beach Arlington. In 1961, Ron DiMenna opened "The Original" Ron Jon Surf Shop in Ship Bottom, putting East Coast surfing on the map. Vacationers today can catch the Nerds and other bands playing at Joe Pop's Shore Bar and enjoy dinner at various spots, including Ship Bottom Shellfish, Baker's Port Hole, and Raimondo's to name a few.

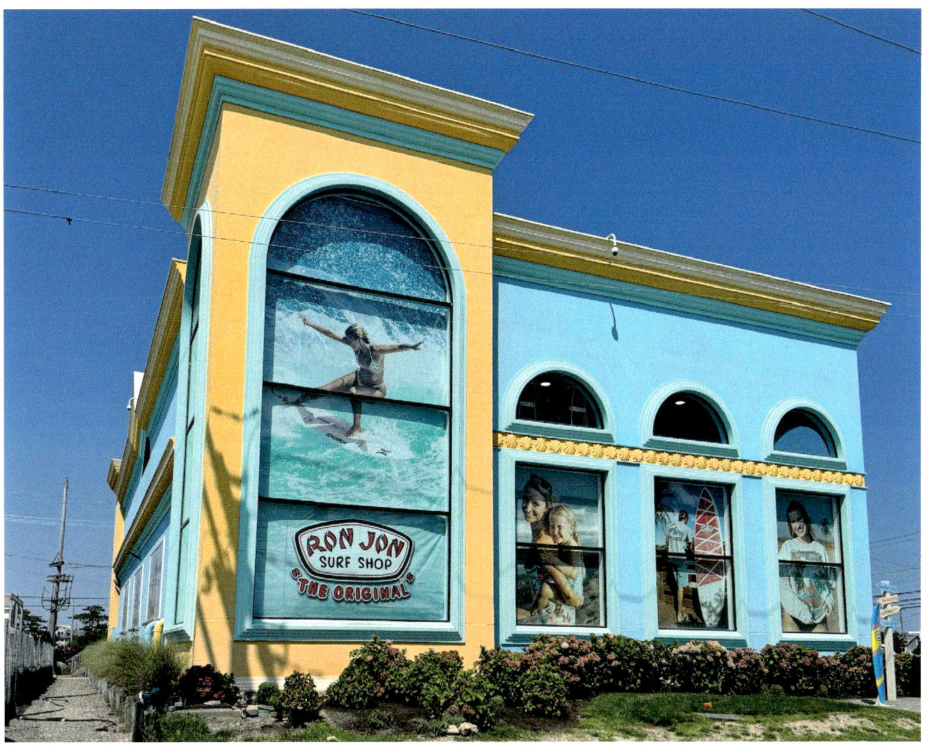

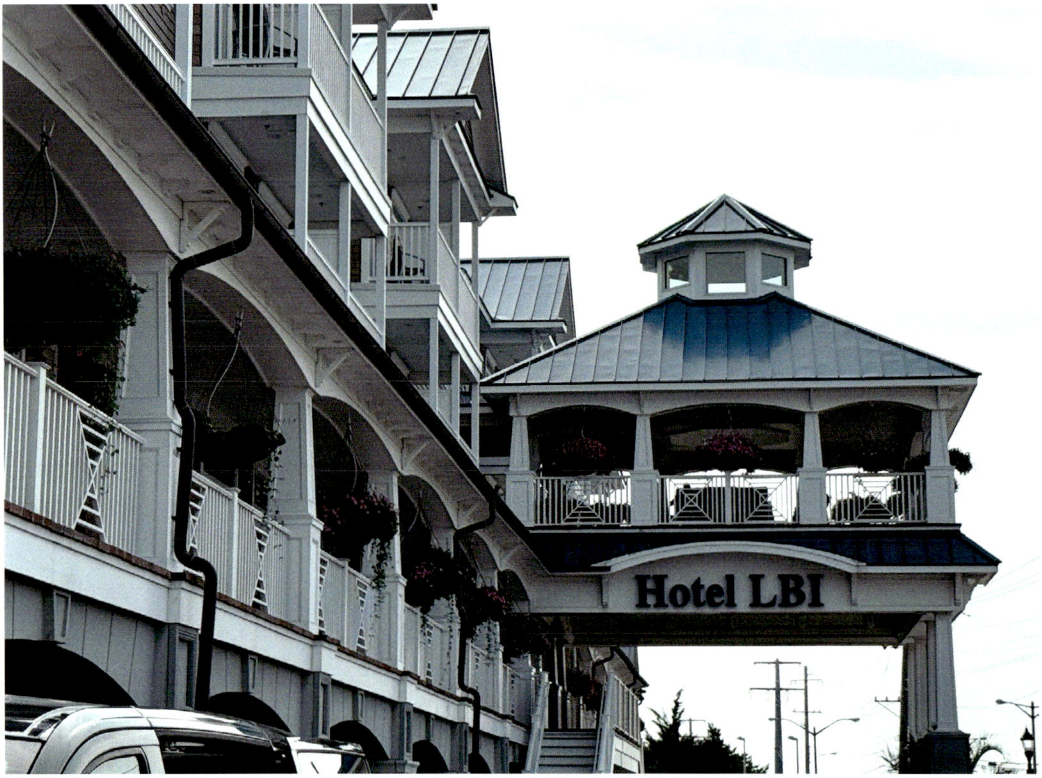

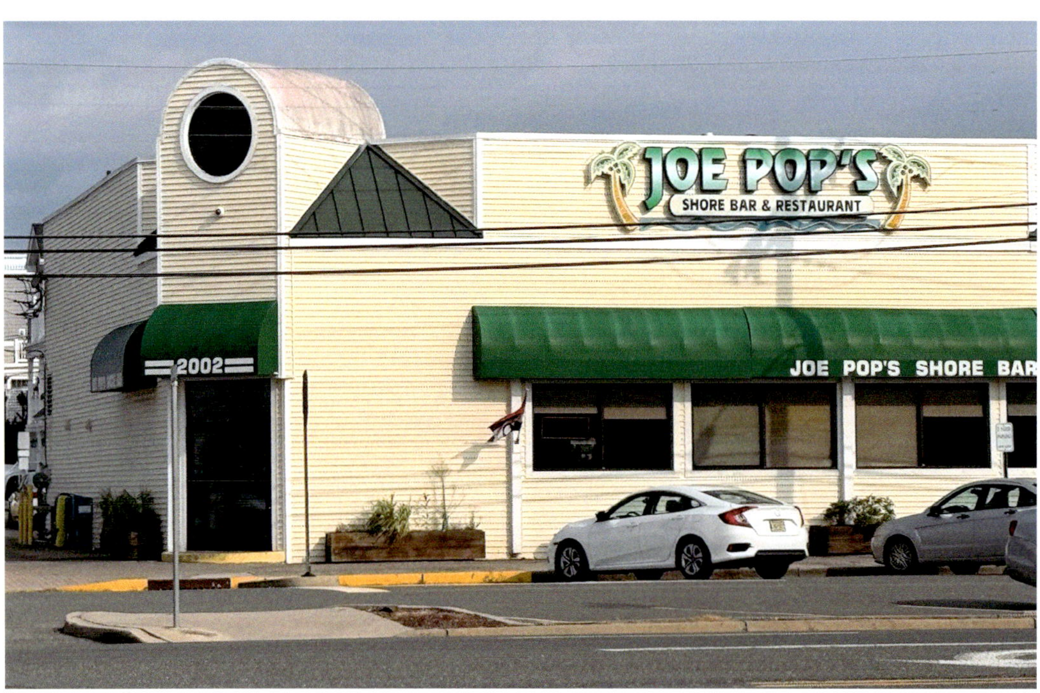
Hotel LBI
JOE POP'S
SHORE BAR & RESTAURANT
2002
JOE POP'S SHORE BAR

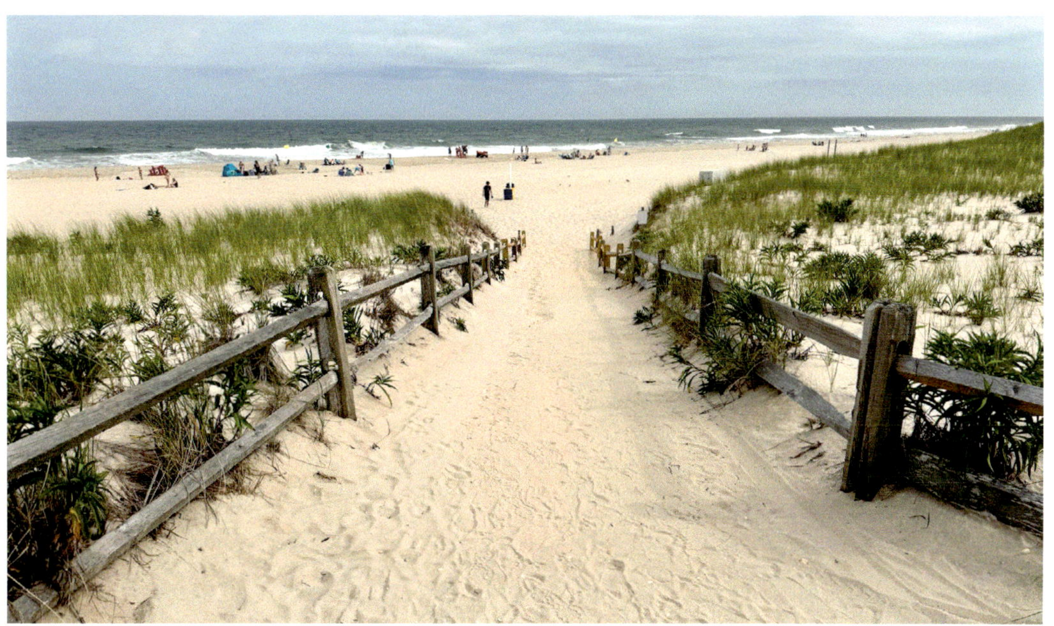

BEACH HAVEN

Incorporated: 1890
Motto: The Queen City
Origin of the name: Named by founder Archelaus Pharo's daughter
Formed from: Portions of Eagleswood Township
Previous names: Beach Heaven

In the mid-nineteenth century, wealthy businessmen from Philadelphia and the surrounding South Jersey areas would visit the Long Beach House in present-day Holgate to hunt and fish. Some of them, including Archelaus Pharo, wanted to create their own vacation community, and chose land just to the north which would eventually become Beach Haven. The Engleside Hotel was constructed in 1876 and stood until the 1940s when it was demolished; the current Engleside Inn stands close to the original site. Several wooden shingle baymen's cottages were built in the area around this time, complimenting the towns Victorian, Edwardian, and Queen Anne charm. On the evening of July 1, 1916, an Engleside Hotel guest went for a swim and was attacked by a large shark, he would later succumb to his injuries in the hotel office. This was the first of five attacks on the Jerey Shore during the summer of 1916, which served as inspiration for Peter Benchley's *Jaws*. Like other LBI communities, parts of Beach Haven were destroyed during the storms of 1944 and 1962. Today, Beach Haven is the center of action on LBI, with plenty of shoppes, restaurants and bars, including the Black Whale, Buckalews, Tuckers Tavern, Bird & Betty's, the Sea Shell, and the Hudson House aka the HUD (technically in Long Beach Township). Beach Haven is also home to Fantasy Island Amusement Park and Bay Village, making it a well-rounded family resort.

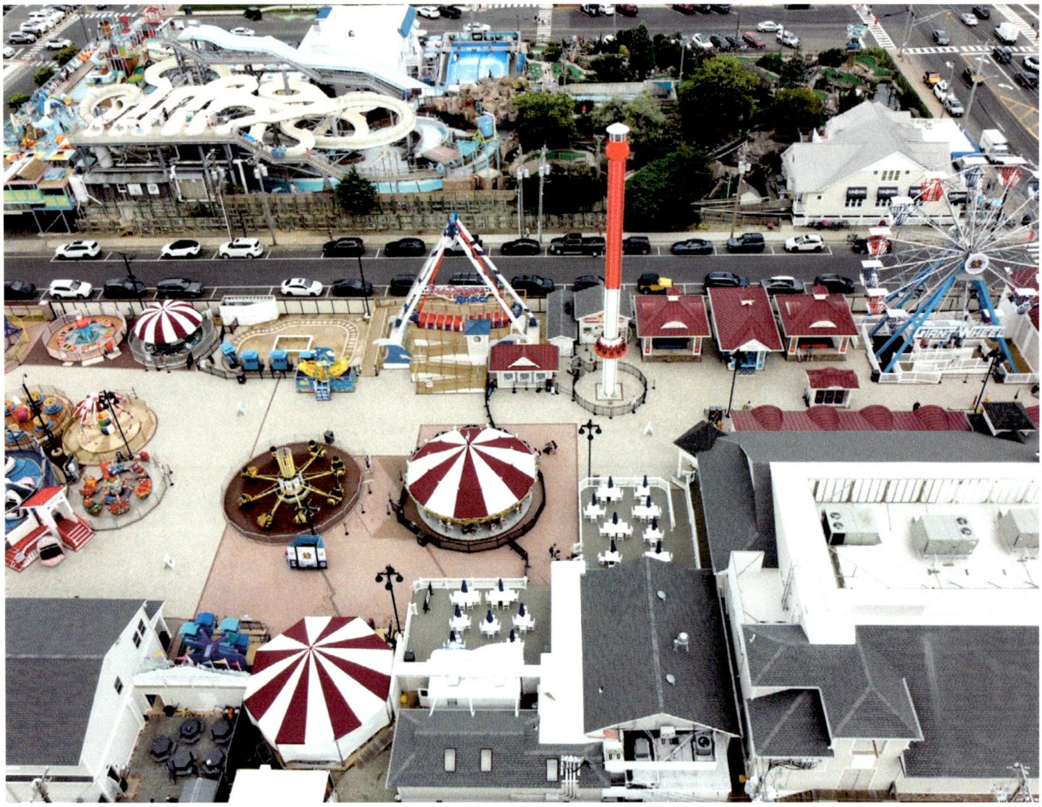

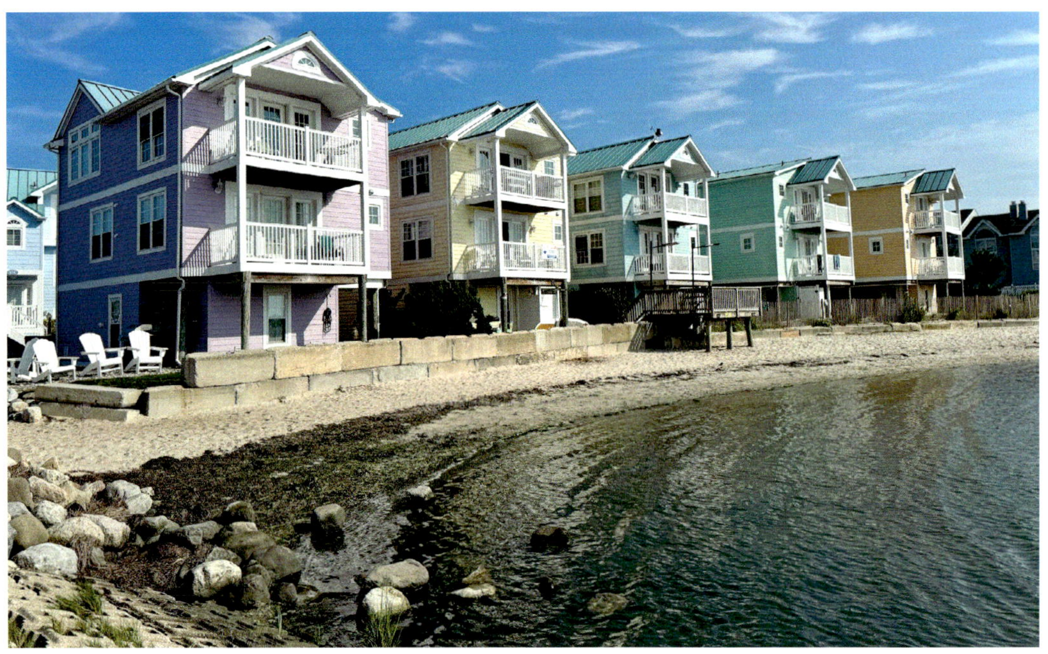

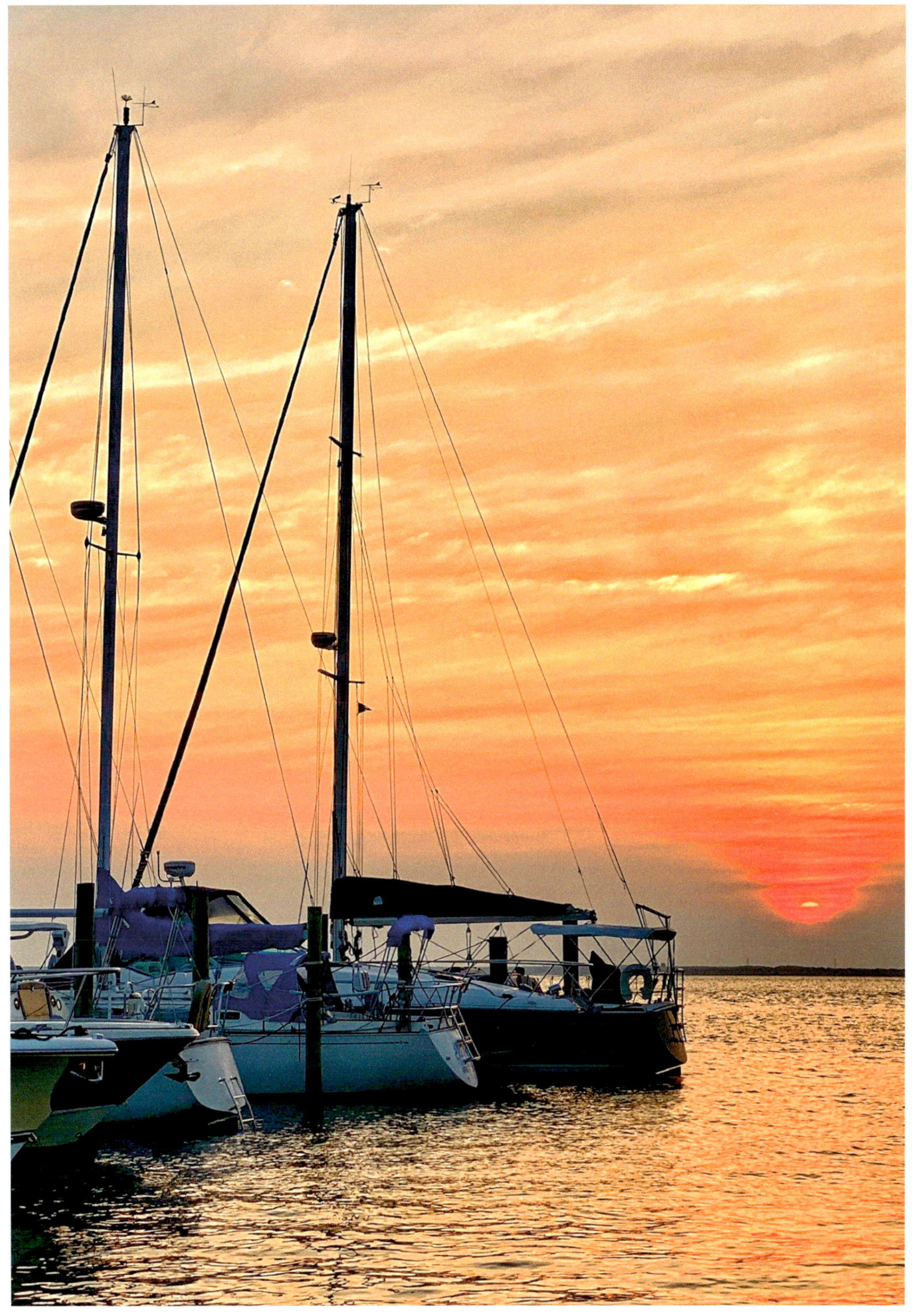

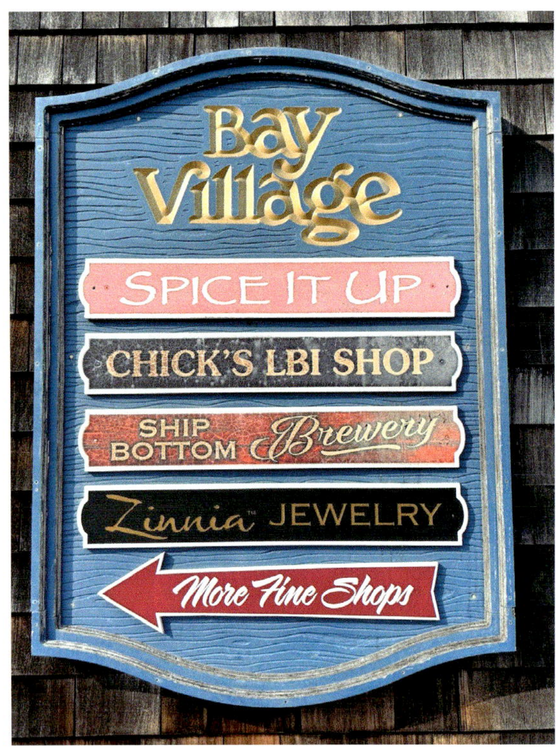
Bay
Village
SPICE IT UP
CHICK'S LBI SHOP
SHIP BOTTOM Brewery
Zinnia JEWELRY
More Fine Shops

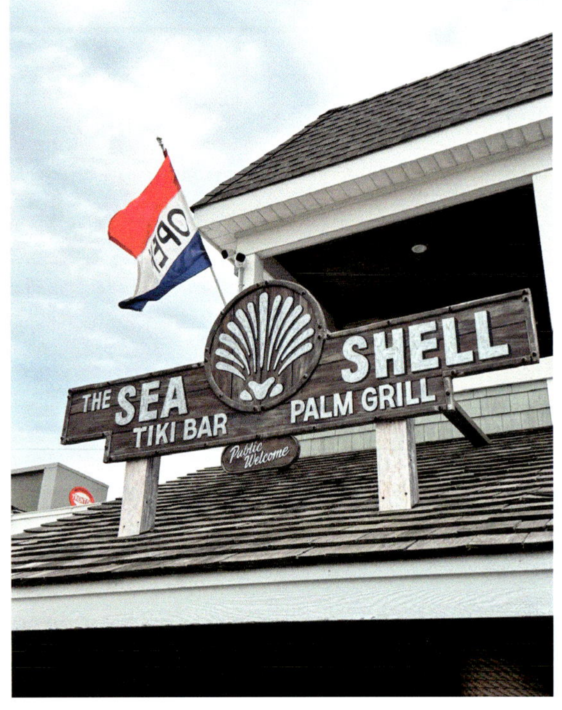
OPEN
THE SEA SHELL
TIKI BAR PALM GRILL
Public Welcome

LONG BEACH TOWNSHIP

Incorporated: 1899
Motto: None
Origin of the name: named for the length of the island along the bay
Formed from: Portions of Eagleswood Township, Little Egg Harbor Township, Ocean Township, Stafford Township and Union Township

By the end of the nineteenth century, the towns of Beach Haven, Harvey Cedars, and Surf City were already established. At the time, most of the other smaller communities on LBI were governed by the mainland towns of Eagleswood, Barnegat, or Stafford Township. In 1899, Long Beach Township was created to help organize many of these smaller towns into one municipality. Worth mentioning here are the histories of these three towns:

Loveladies: This community was named for prominent fisherman Thomas Lovelady, whose surname was also applied to the Lovelady's Island Life Saving Station. In the 1940s, it was known as Long Beach Park but reverted back to Loveladies in 1952 to avoid confusion with other parts of the island.

Brant Beach: This quiet stretch of land south of Ship Bottom was named after the large number of Brant Geese in the area. In 1926, the Ockanickon Hotel opened, which was later renamed Wida's Brant Beach Hotel. Today it operates as Daddy O Hotel and Restaurant.

Holgate: James Holgate established this community in the early 1900s when he purchased land south of Beach Haven all the way to the southern tip of LBI. At the time, sportsmen and wealthy vacationers enjoyed stays at the Long Beach House, originally built in 1815 as the Philadelphia Company House, and later renamed the Bond Hotel in the 1850s. Edwin Forsythe National Wildlife Refuge occupies the lower portion of Holgate.

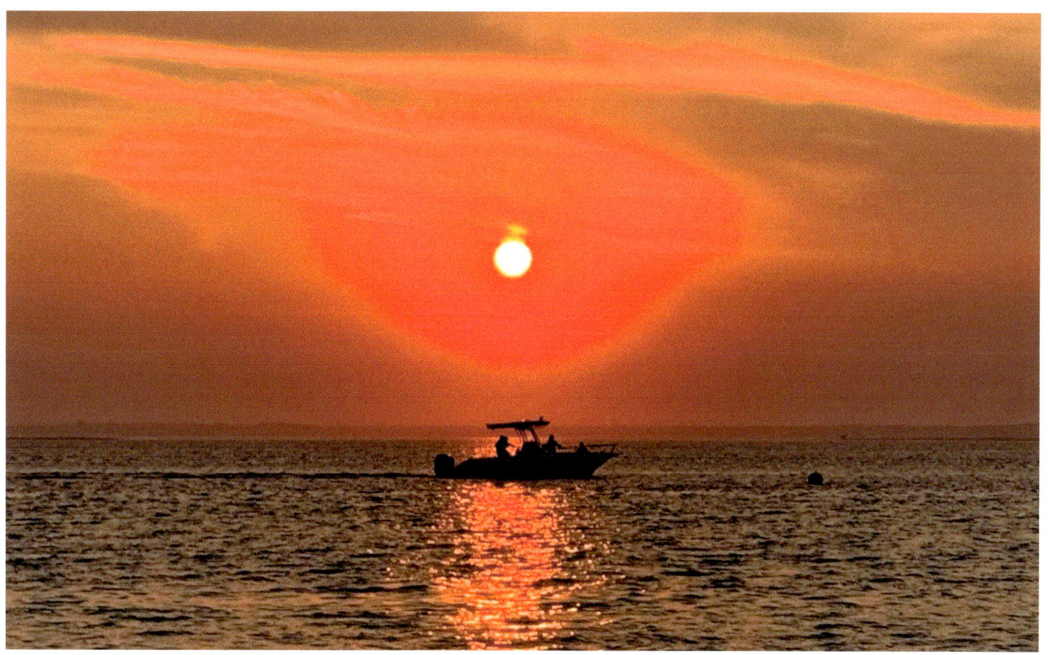

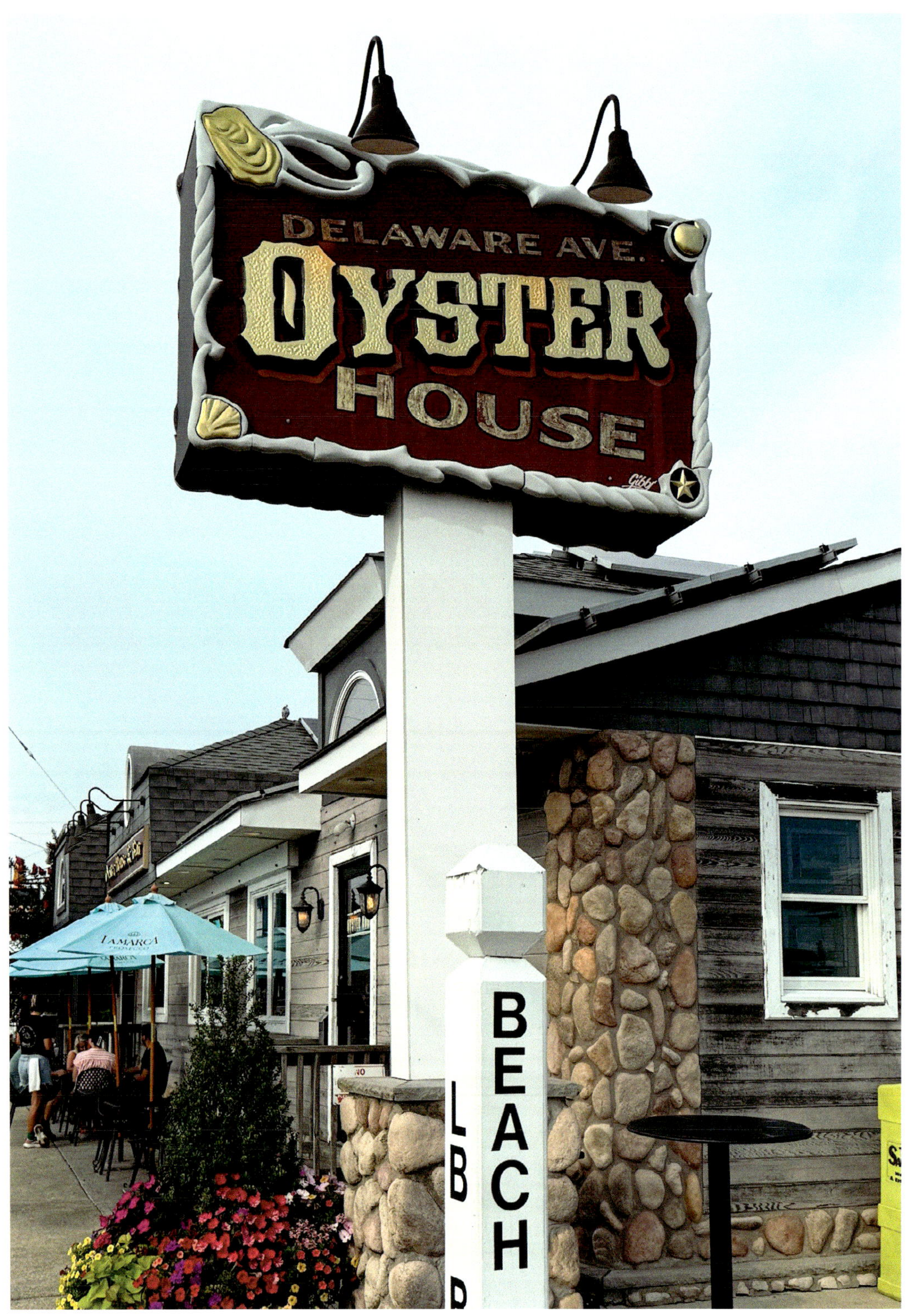

DELAWARE AVE.
OYSTER
HOUSE
Gibby
BEACH
LB

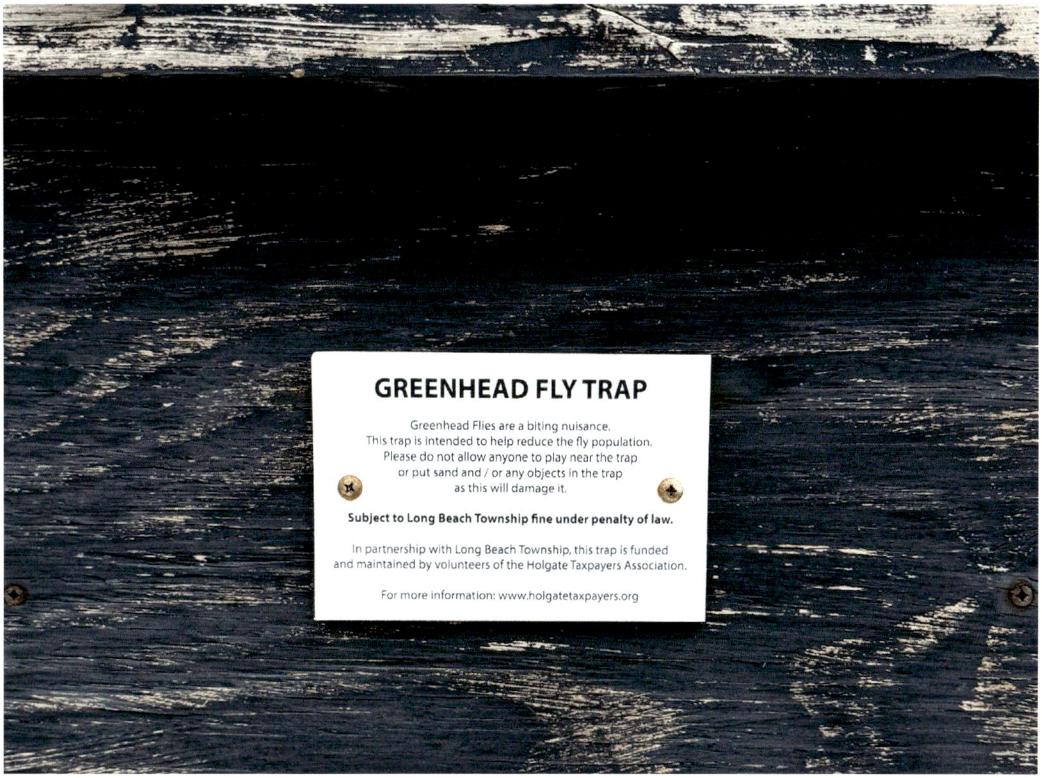

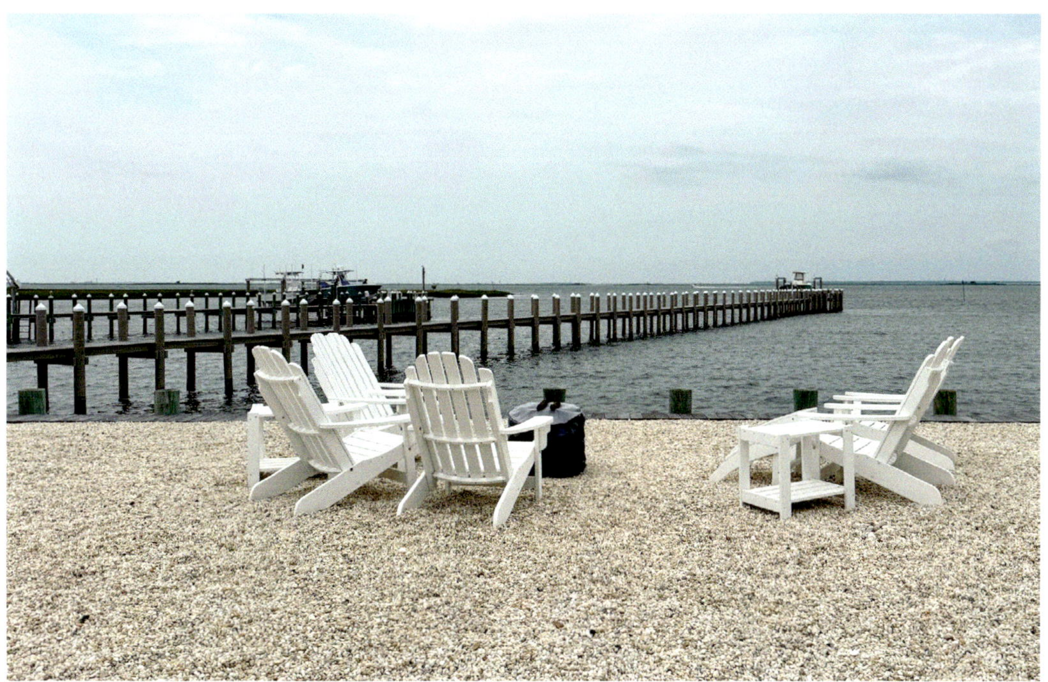
GREENHEAD FLY TRAP

Greenhead Flies are a biting nuisance.
This trap is intended to help reduce the fly population.
Please do not allow anyone to play near the trap
or put sand and / or any objects in the trap
as this will damage it.

Subject to Long Beach Township fine under penalty of law.

In partnership with Long Beach Township, this trap is funded
and maintained by volunteers of the Holgate Taxpayers Association.

For more information: www.holgatetaxpayers.org

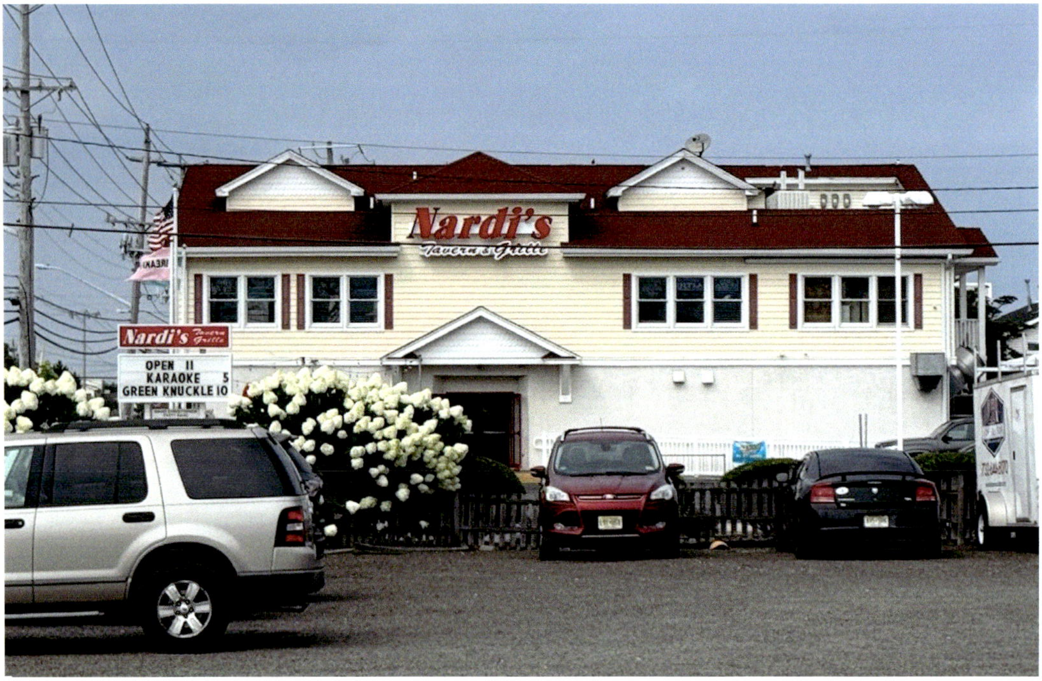

Nardi's
Tavern & Grill
Nardi's
Tavern & Grille
OPEN 11
KARAOKE 5
GREEN KNUCKLE 10

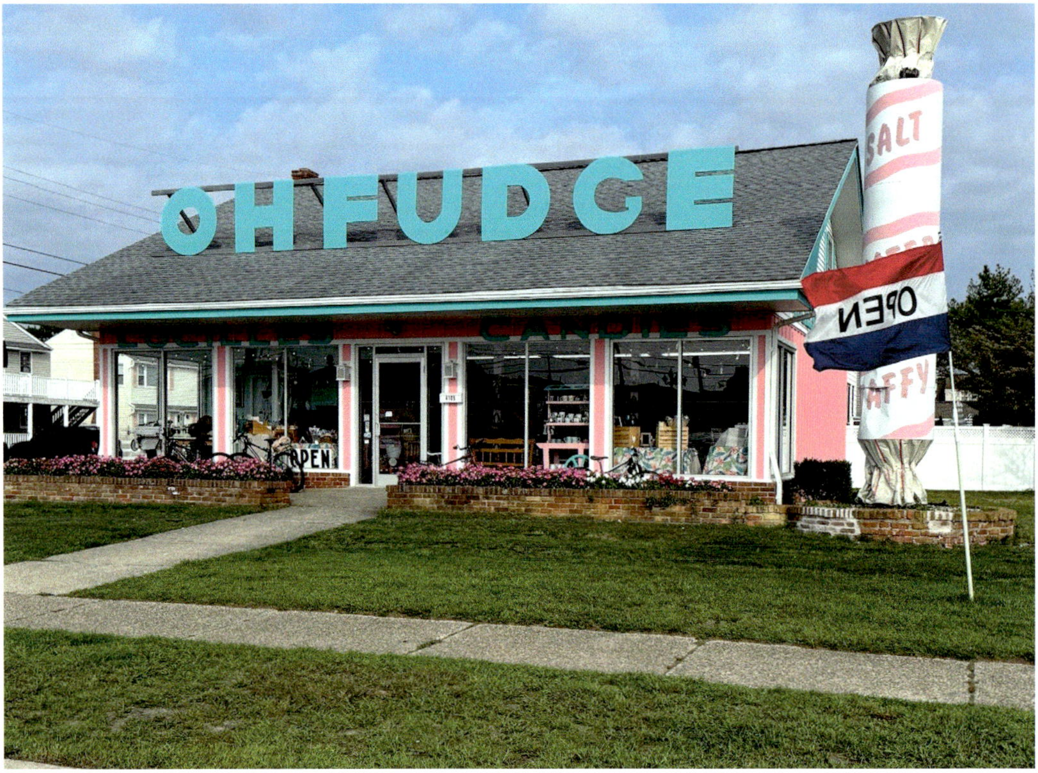

OH FUDGE
SALT
OPEN
TAFFY
OPEN

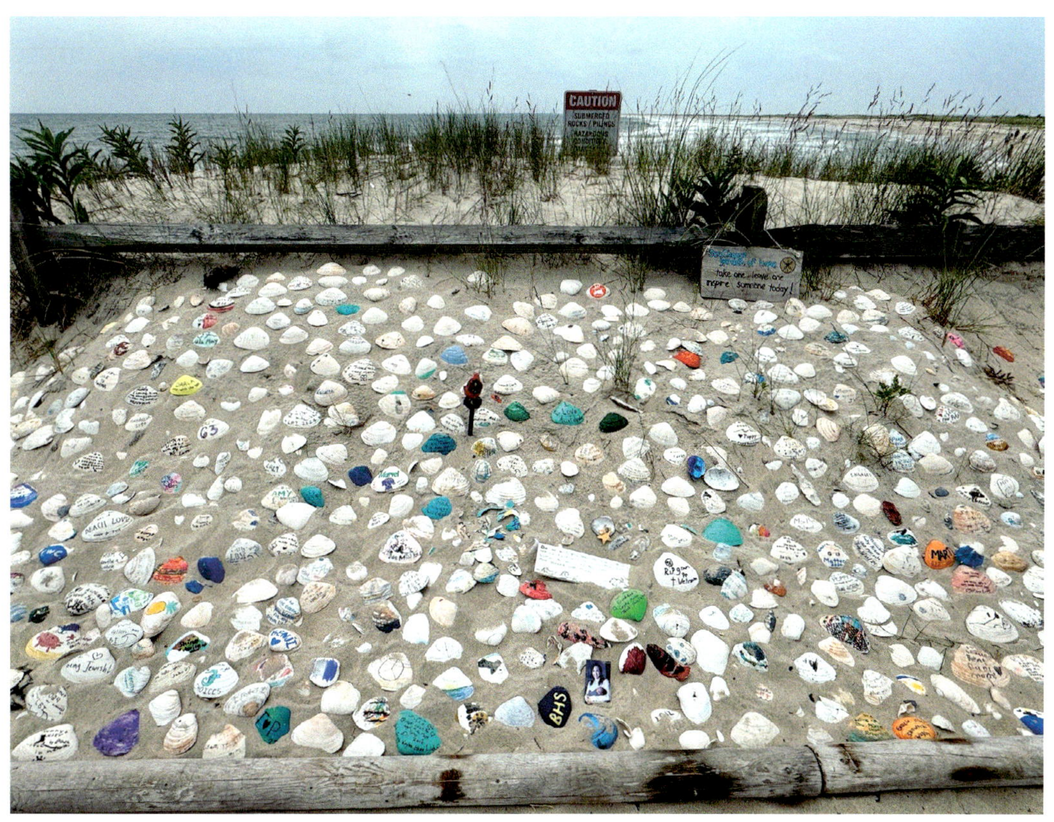

* * * * * *

To continue the journey south, be sure to check out "volume two" of this book:
Ocean Access: The Beachfront Towns of Atlantic & Cape May County, New Jersey.

SELECT BIBLIOGRAPHY

en.wikipedia.org/wiki/Sandy_Hook

www.nps.gov/gate/learn/historyculture/upload/SAHOLightBull-13August2015_rev9April2018.pdf

www.nps.gov/gate/learn/historyculture/hancock.htm

en.wikipedia.org/wiki/Middletown_Township,_New_Jersey

en.wikipedia.org/wiki/Board_of_Fortifications

www.monmouthbeachlife.com/sea-bright/normandie-hotel-sb-spent-splendor/

en.wikipedia.org/wiki/Sea_Bright,_New_Jersey#History

www.monmouthbeachlife.com/sea-bright/nauvoo-start-of-sea-bright/#:~:text=The%20Freehold%20
physician%20bought%20from,became%20an%20official%2C%20independent%20borough.

www.monmouthbeachlife.com/just-beyond-mb/the-railroads-of-sb-mb-and-lb/

www.monmouthbeachlife.com/mb-history/bathing-pavilion-history/

en.wikipedia.org/wiki/Monmouth_Beach,_New_Jersey

www.monmouthbeachlife.com/mb-history/monmouth-beach-rich-and-famous/

en.wikipedia.org/wiki/Long_Branch,_New_Jersey

www.monmouthbeachlife.com/long-branch/boardwalk-pier-history/#:~:text=Long%20Branch%20
Ocean%20Pier%2C%201880,%2C%202017%20(MAC%20Photography)

www.monmouthbeachlife.com/long-branch/beginnings-of-long-branch/

en.wikipedia.org/wiki/Deal,_New_Jersey

www.usatoday.com/story/news/nation/2014/11/15/tragic-shipwreck-still-remembered-along-jersey-
shore/19101615/

en.wikipedia.org/wiki/Allenhurst,_New_Jersey#History

www.app.com/story/news/local/eatontown-asbury-park/allenhurst/2014/08/31/allenhurst-beach-
club-dyes-ocean-green/14910945/

en.wikipedia.org/wiki/Ocean_Grove,_New_Jersey#History

www.oceangrove.org/history

en.wikipedia.org/wiki/Bradley_Beach,_New_Jersey

www.bradleybeachnj.gov/about/#:~:text=A%20HISTORY%20OF%20BRADLEY%20

BEACH,a%20natural%20haven%20for%20waterfowl

www.avonbytheseanj.com/community/about_avon_by_the_sea/history_of_avon.php

www.belmar.com/useruploads/files/Belmar_ERI.pdf

en.wikipedia.org/wiki/Spring_Lake,_New_Jersey

www.springlakeboro.org/history.html

www.springlakehistoricalsociety.org/history

www.seagirt-nj.gov/home/about/pages/history

en.wikipedia.org/wiki/Manasquan,_New_Jersey

www.monmouthcountyclerk.com/archives/record-groups/municipal-records/manasquan/

www.manasquan-nj.gov/borough-historian/pages/history-continued

en.wikipedia.org/wiki/Point_Pleasant_Beach,_New_Jersey#History

www.pointpleasantbeach.org/243/History-of-Point-Pleasant-Beach

jenkinsons.com/history/

en.wikipedia.org/wiki/Bay_Head,_New_Jersey

www.mantoloking.org/our-community/pages/history

en.wikipedia.org/wiki/Mantoloking,_New_Jersey

www.thecitypulse.com/post/mantoloking-newest-mansions-on-the-rise-10-years-after-superstorm-sandy

www.bricktownship.net/government/town-history/

en.wikipedia.org/wiki/Brick_Township,_New_Jersey

en.wikipedia.org/wiki/Dover_Beaches_North,_New_Jersey#History

www.lavallette.org/history.html

www.lavallette.org/history.html

en.wikipedia.org/wiki/Dover_Beaches_South,_New_Jersey#:~:text=History,-Starlight%20Motel%20(since&text=The%20current%20location%20of%20Ortley,now%20Route%2035%20in%201913

www.discoverseasideheights.com/history/boardwalk-history

en.wikipedia.org/wiki/Seaside_Park,_New_Jersey

www.seasideparknj.org/history/#:~:text=Seaside%20Park%20was%20a%20section,Park%20began%20to%20slowly%20grow

en.wikipedia.org/wiki/Island_Beach_State_Park

www.islandbeachnj.org/History/History.html

en.wikipedia.org/wiki/Barnegat_Light,_New_Jersey

www.harveycedars.org/cn/webpage.cfm?tpid=14777

en.wikipedia.org/wiki/Harvey_Cedars,_New_Jersey

www.hmdb.org/m.asp?m=209202

shipbottom.org/history-2/

nj.gov/dep/hpo/hrrcn_sandy_OCE_GB_147_148_PDF/OCE_GB_148_v35.pdf

beachhaven-nj.gov/resources/history-of-beach-haven/

www.bay-magazine.com/single-post/2018/07/01/the-towns-of-long-beach-island-old-and-new

ABOUT THE AUTHOR

Born and raised in Belleville, New Jersey, Rich Romano currently lives in Wayne with his wife and two sons. An avid historian and photographer, Rich enjoys visiting, researching, and writing about New Jersey and New York's most historic and interesting places, as depicted in his first two books, *Forgotten New Jersey* and *Death Island: The Grim Past and Modern Renewal of Roosevelt Island*. His next book is the second part of *Ocean Access*, featuring the beachfront towns of Atlantic and Cape May County.

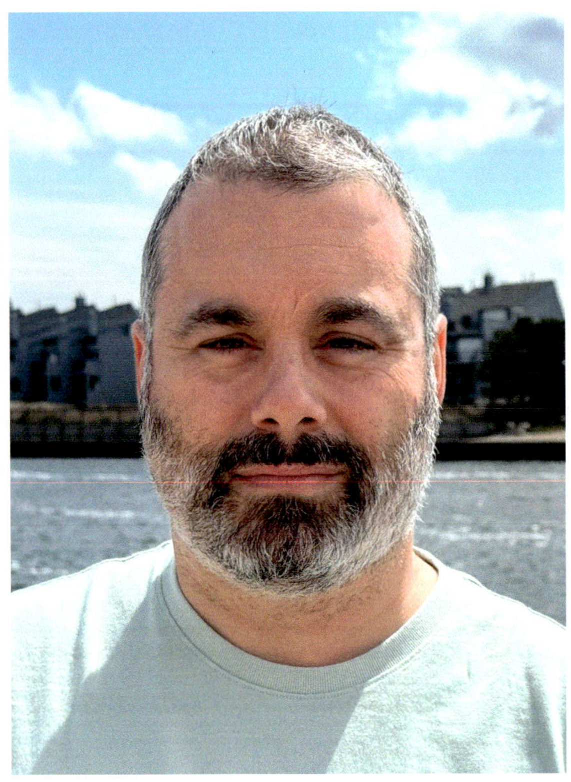